THE LUNGS AND BREATHING

Brian R. Ward

Series Consultant
Dr Alan Maryon-Davis
MB, BChir, MSc, MRCP, FFCM

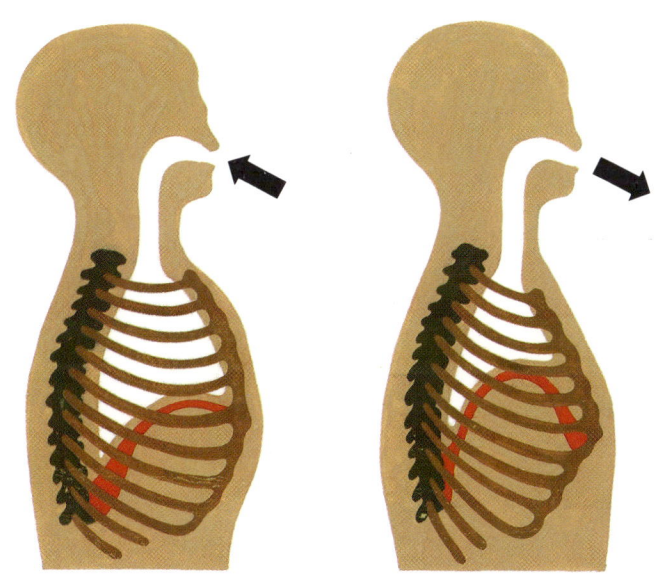

Franklin Watts
London • New York • Toronto • Sydney

© **1988 Franklin Watts**
Original edition first published in 1982
Franklin Watts
12a Golden Square
London W1

Published in the United States by
Franklin Watts Inc.
387 Park Avenue South
New York, NY 10016

Published in Australia by
Franklin Watts Australia
14 Mars Road
Lane Cove
NSW 2066

ISBN: 0 86313 706 7

Illustrations: Marion Appleton, Howard Dyke, David Mallott,
Charles Raymond

Photographs: Christian Bonnington 45. Health Education Authority
33: Superman is the trade mark of DC Comics Inc. © 1982. Used
by the Health Education Authority under licence. All rights reserved.
Science Photo Library 24. Science Photo Library: CNRI 7, 11, 27;
Martin Dohrn 1, 23; Dr George Gornacz 43; Eric Grave 20;
Harvey Pincis 35; Dr Gary Settles 29; James Stevenson 31.
Zefa Picture Library 13, 19, 30, 39, 40.

Printed in Belgium

Contents

Introduction

All the **cells** of the body need **oxygen** so that they can live, grow and produce energy for the body's activities. This colourless gas is present in the air we breathe, and it is the function of the **lungs** to extract oxygen from the air, to transfer it to the blood where it can be carried to the cells of the body.

Living cells produce **carbon dioxide**, another colourless gas, as a waste product. The lungs remove this gas from the blood before it can build up to harmful levels.

The passage of the air in and out of the lungs also serves other important functions. Air passing through the nose allows us to have a sense of smell, and also takes part in the sensation of taste.

We also use the air currents in the throat to generate sound, so that we can talk.

Yet another function of breathing is to regulate the amount of water present in the system and to help cool the body.

The whole breathing apparatus, or **respiratory system**, is one of the main life-support systems of the body. Its structure consists of a pair of sponge-like lungs in the chest, supplied by branching air pipes connecting with the mouth and nose. The lungs have a very large blood supply, and nearly half of the heart's output is pumped to the lungs to collect oxygen on its way to the rest of the body. The heart and lungs are protected in the chest by the bony structure of the rib cage.

▷ The respiratory system consists of the lungs and airways and, together with the circulatory system (heart and blood vessels), is responsible for supplying oxygen to all parts of the body. This is one of the most important mechanisms in the body. The main organs of breathing are located in the chest cavity, protected by the rib cage.

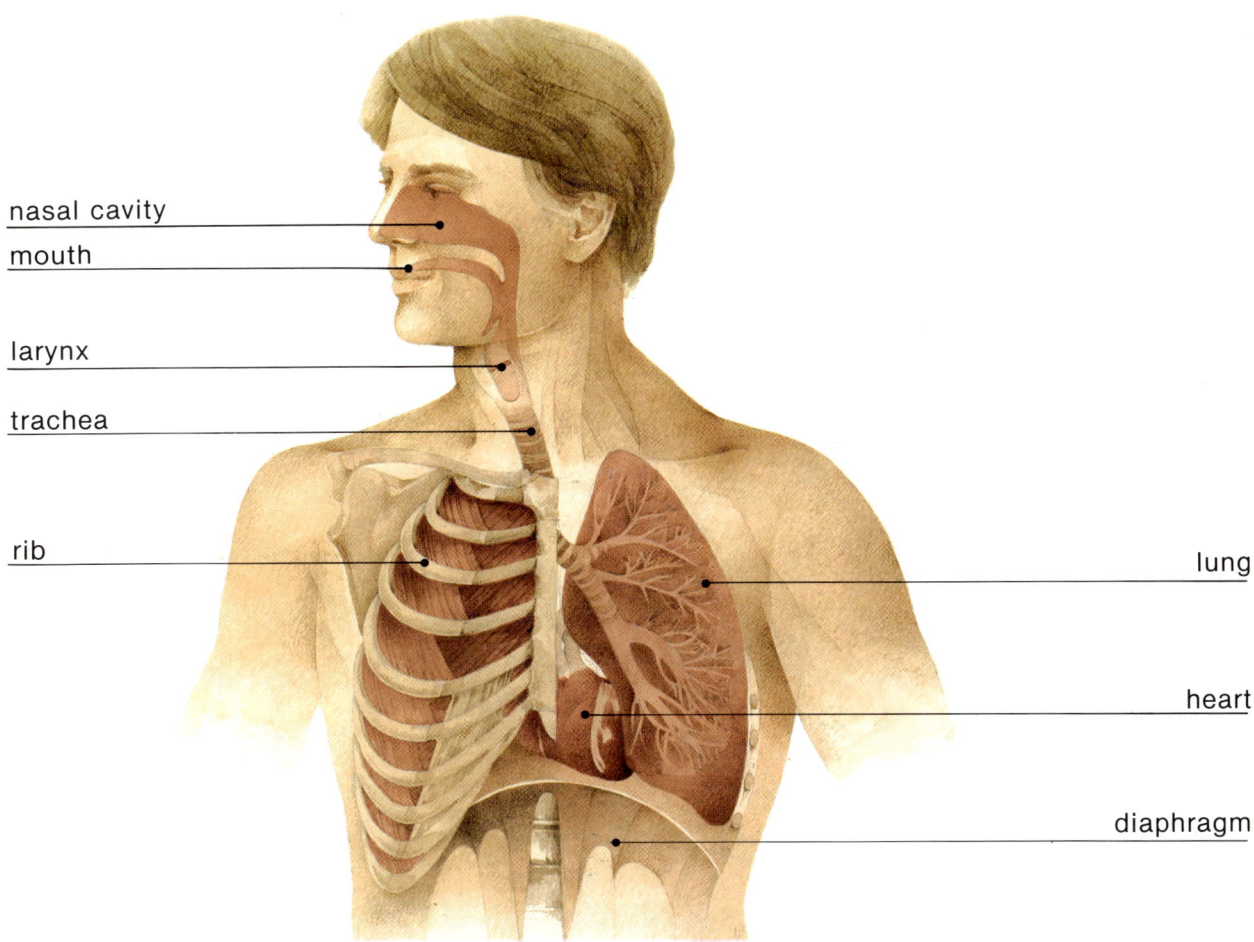

nasal cavity

mouth

larynx

trachea

rib

lung

heart

diaphragm

The air we breathe

- A newborn baby takes about 40 breaths per minute.
- A 1-year-old takes about 24 breaths per minute.
- An adult takes about 14 breaths per minute.
- An adult normally takes in about 7 litres (12 pints) of air per minute. If he or she is exercising, air intake leaps to about 100 litres (22 gall) per minute.
- Each day an adult takes in about 15 cu m (530 cu ft) of air, or about 400,000 cu m (14 million cu ft) in a lifetime — enough to fill a good-sized oil-tanker.
- The air we breathe in (inspire) is made up of several different gases: oxygen (20%), carbon dioxide (0.04%), nitrogen (78%) and argon (1%), along with very small quantities of other gases.
- Inside the body, the oxygen is used by the cells to produce energy. At the same time, we make carbon dioxide, and this is carried out of the body through the lungs.
- The air we breathe out (or expire) contains less oxygen (only 16%) and more carbon dioxide (4%).
- The amount of nitrogen and argon we inspire and expire stays the same.

The lungs

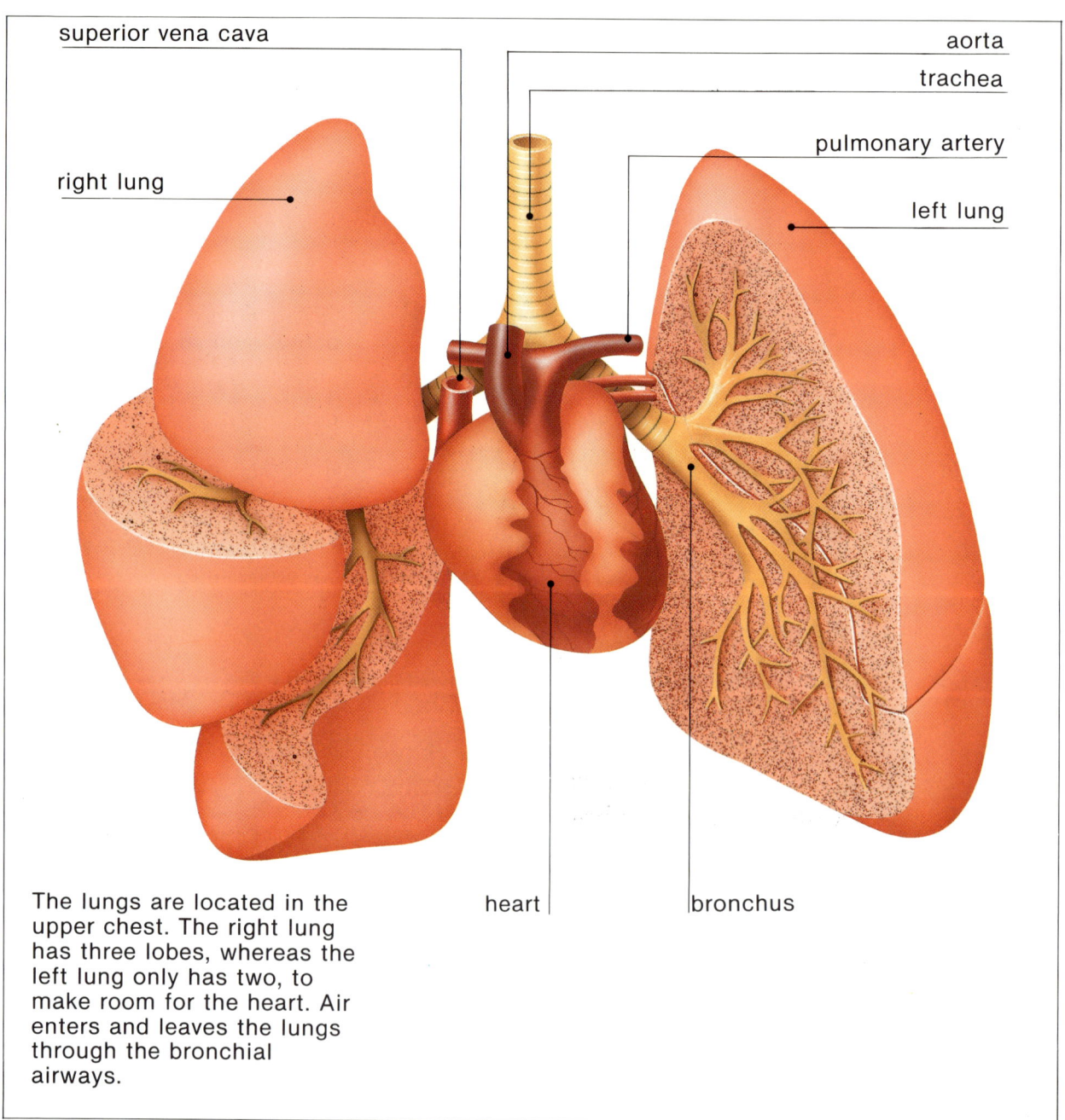

superior vena cava

aorta

trachea

pulmonary artery

right lung

left lung

heart

bronchus

The lungs are located in the upper chest. The right lung has three lobes, whereas the left lung only has two, to make room for the heart. Air enters and leaves the lungs through the bronchial airways.

We have two lungs: large spongy organs located in the chest cavity. They are of slightly different sizes and shapes. The right lung is larger, and is divided into three separate parts. The smaller left lung is in two sections. In an adult, the two lungs together weigh about 1 kg (2.2 lb).

The lungs themselves and the inside of the chest wall are covered with a thin, slippery membrane called the **pleura**. This lets the lungs move about a little as we breathe, sliding without causing damage. The heart fits closely between the lungs near the centre, but slightly to the left of the chest cavity, and its pumping movements against the lungs are also lubricated by the pleura.

The lungs are pale pink in colour in a newborn baby, but they become darker throughout life. This is due to impurities in the air we inhale, some of which cannot be removed by the body's cleaning mechanism and which gradually darken the lungs. In places where there are high levels of air pollution, such as large cities and industrial areas, impurities in the air can cause lung problems, but the main cause of lung disease is smoking.

Before strict industrial health laws existed, the lungs of miners and quarrymen, after a lifetime of inhaling dust, could become hard and stone-like. Only in people such as Eskimos, living in a dust-free environment, do lungs remain pink throughout life.

Lungs are among the last organs to develop properly in an unborn baby. If a baby is born prematurely, before the lungs are fully developed, breathing problems may arise. This is more likely to happen if the mother smokes during pregnancy.

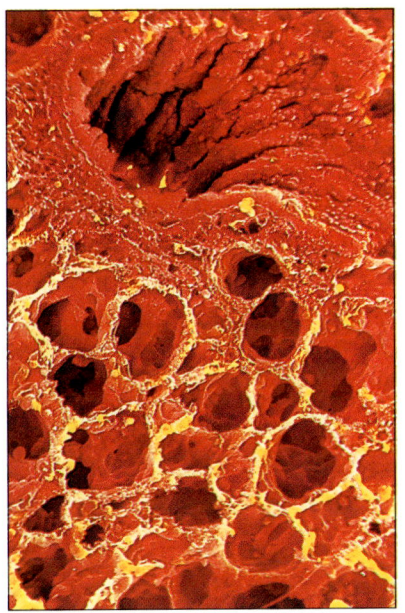

△ This coloured microscope photograph shows the spongy texture of the human lung. At the top of the picture is a bronchiole, one of the smallest airways in the lungs. The smaller circles are **alveoli**, tiny air sacs covered with blood vessels. The yellow areas in the photograph are tissue that connects the alveoli.

The nose and mouth

We can breathe equally well through nose or mouth, although most of the time we breathe through the nose only. Breathing through the mouth is useful when we need extra oxygen during exercise like running.

Air normally enters the paired nostrils and passes into a space called the nasal cavity. This is divided into smaller areas by thin shelves of bone called **nasal conchae**, or **turbinates**. The whole nasal cavity is lined with a thin, moist sheet of **mucous membrane**, and has a large blood supply. The nasal cavity serves to clean the air we breathe, because large inhaled particles stick to the mucous membrane. Here, too, cold air is warmed before passing to the lungs, and a patch of special tissue detects odours present in the air.

More air spaces called **sinuses** open into the nasal cavity. These sometimes become inflamed and blocked, causing **sinusitis**.

Air leaves the nasal cavity and enters the **pharynx**, or throat, on its way to the lungs. A flap called the **uvula** hangs down at the back of the soft **palate**, which can seal off the nasal cavity or the airway through the mouth.

The lips and tongue play no direct part in breathing, except in aiding the soft palate to shut off the air flow through the mouth, during swallowing. Snoring is caused by air forcing its way past the soft palate when a sleeping person breathes partly through the mouth.

▷ The nose, mouth and throat have several functions. They take part in breathing, warming the air as it enters the body and cleaning the airways. They are also involved in chewing, swallowing, speech and the senses of smell and taste.

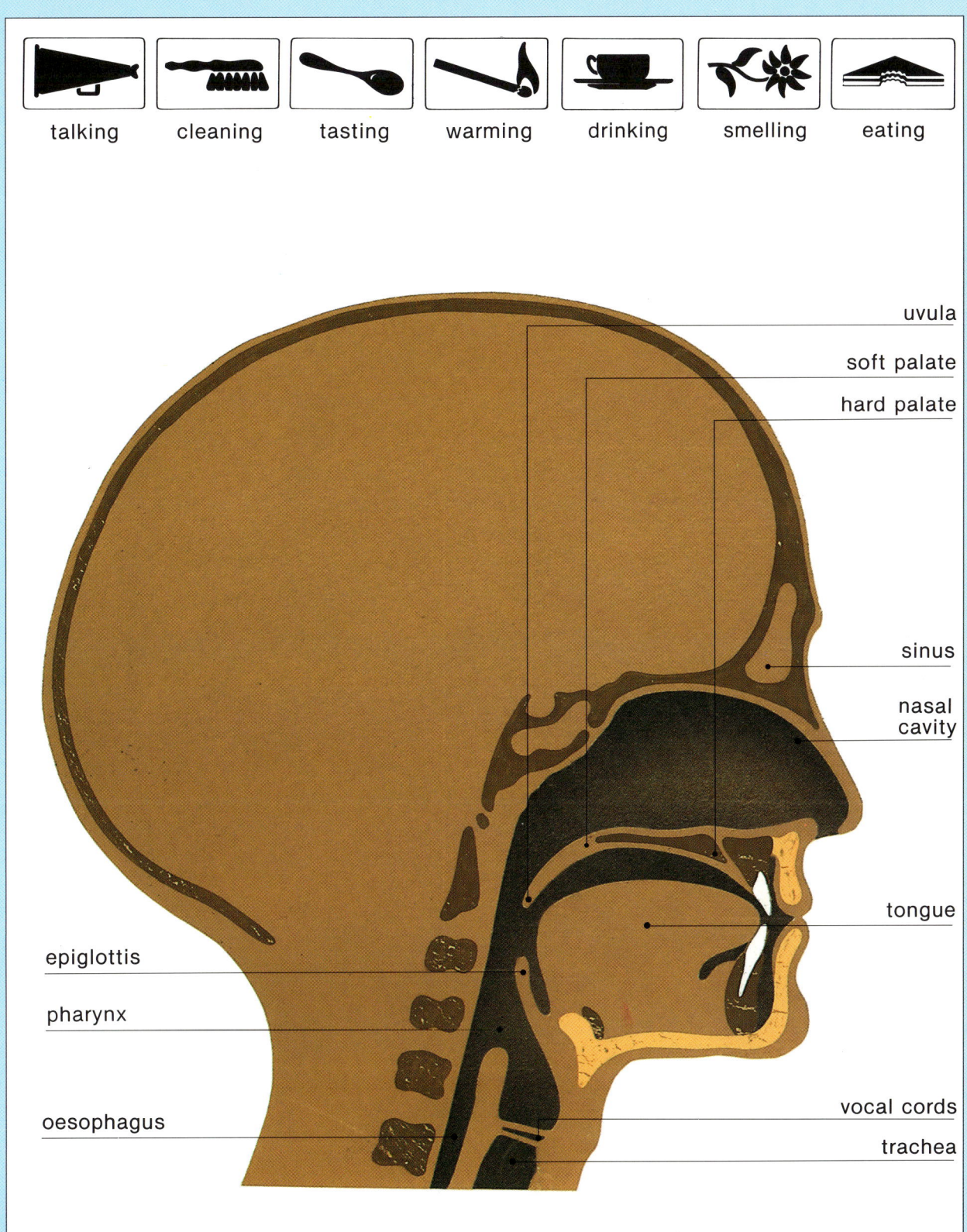

talking   cleaning   tasting   warming   drinking   smelling   eating

uvula

soft palate

hard palate

sinus

nasal cavity

tongue

epiglottis

pharynx

vocal cords

trachea

oesophagus

The bronchial tree

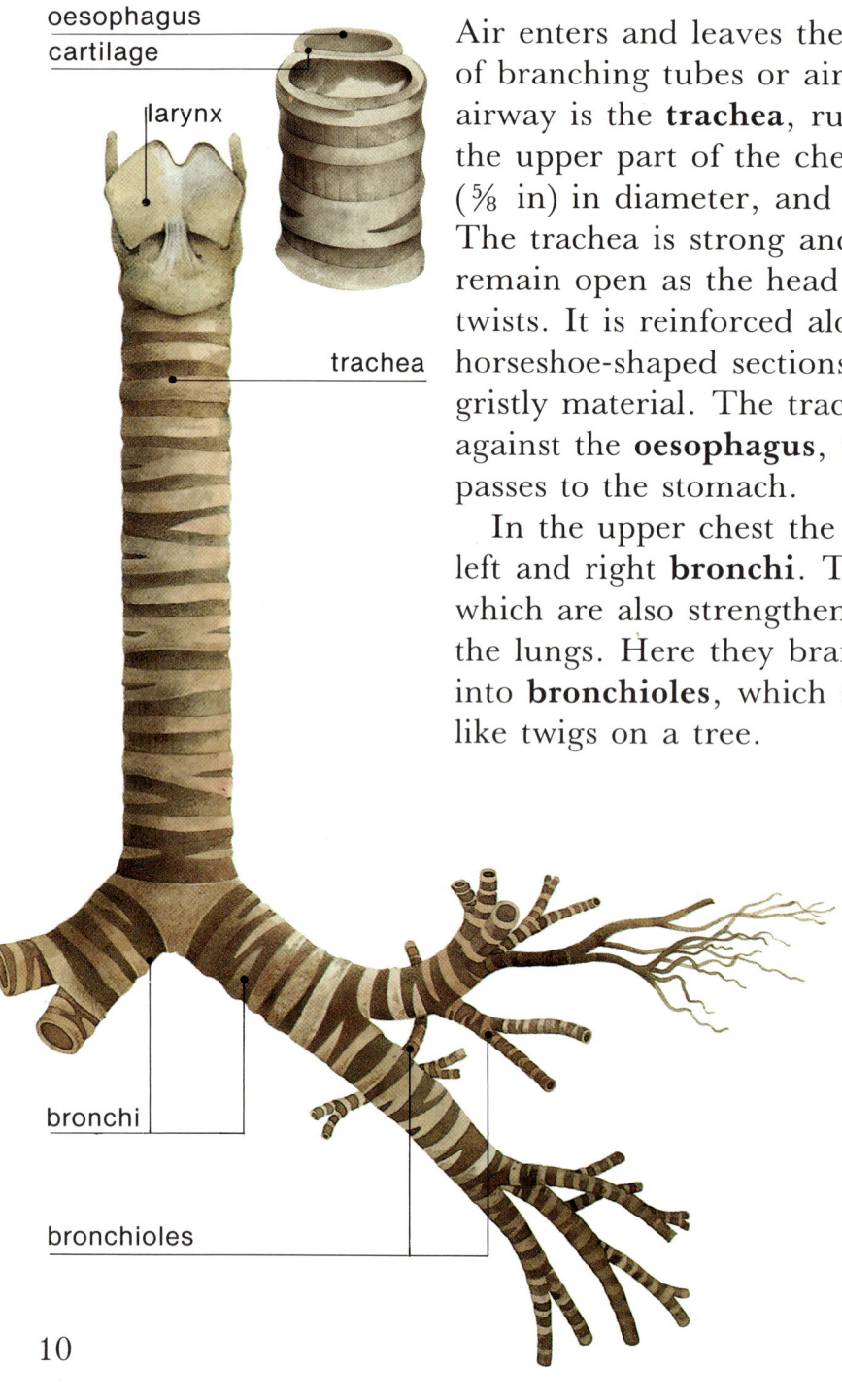

oesophagus
cartilage
larynx
trachea
bronchi
bronchioles

Air enters and leaves the lungs through a system of branching tubes or airways. The largest airway is the **trachea**, running from the throat to the upper part of the chest. It is about 1.5 cm (⅝ in) in diameter, and 10 cm (4 in) in length. The trachea is strong and flexible, so it can remain open as the head is moved and the neck twists. It is reinforced along its length by many horseshoe-shaped sections of **cartilage**, a tough, gristly material. The trachea is pressed tightly against the **oesophagus**, through which food passes to the stomach.

In the upper chest the trachea branches into left and right **bronchi**. These two short tubes, which are also strengthened with cartilage, enter the lungs. Here they branch again and again, into **bronchioles**, which spread through the lungs like twigs on a tree.

◁ The airways to the lungs have a branching structure. At the top of the bronchial tree is the trachea (windpipe), which is held rigid by horseshoe-shaped pieces of cartilage. The oesophagus passes down behind the trachea. At the other end of the bronchial tree, the tiny bronchioles branch into "twigs", carrying air to all parts of the lungs.

The smallest bronchioles are about 1 mm (0·04 in) in diameter. They differ from the larger airways in having no cartilage to support their walls. Instead, they have strands of smooth muscle wound around them. These can contract to narrow the tubular bronchioles and restrict the flow of air. The whole "bronchial tree", consisting of the trachea, bronchi and bronchioles, is lined with moist mucous membrane. In the lining of the larger airways are **goblet cells**, which produce **mucus** to keep the surface moist, and hair-like **cilia**, which help to keep the system clean.

△ This coloured X-ray clearly shows the branching structure of the airways to the lungs. This is why the system is called the "bronchial tree". Here, the lungs appear blue, the ribs show up in green, and the trachea, bronchi and bronchioles are red.

The diaphragm

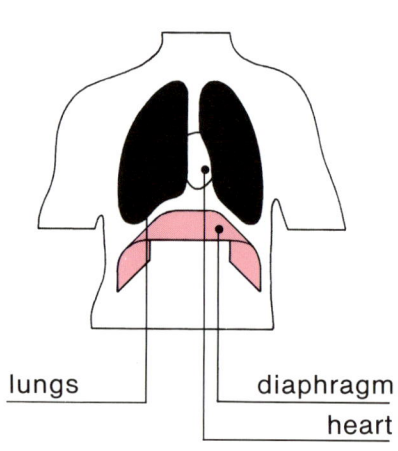

lungs   diaphragm

heart

△ The diaphragm is a sheet of muscle at the floor of the rib cage. When it is relaxed, it is dome-shaped, but when it contracts, it flattens out.

The lungs fill the chest cavity, which is formed by the rib cage. The ribs protect the heart and lungs from damage, and are important in deep breathing.

The floor of the chest cavity is formed by the **diaphragm**. This is a strong sheet made up from criss-crossed layers of muscle, and separates the contents of the chest – the heart and lungs – from the organs in the abdomen. The stomach and liver fit just below the diaphragm. Large blood vessels such as the **aorta** and the **vena cava** pass through the diaphragm, together with the oesophagus.

At the front of the body, the diaphragm follows the curved line of the bottom of the rib cage. Deeper in the chest, it curves even more, into a bell shape. Tough supporting **ligaments** help to keep the diaphragm from overstretching when its muscles are relaxed.

When the diaphragm muscles shorten, or contract, the diaphragm flattens and moves lower in the chest, allowing the lungs to expand when they fill with air. This movement is the basis of normal quiet breathing.

Nerves supplying the diaphragm and other organs in the abdomen are spread out just below the ribs. If a person is struck violently in the abdomen, the action of these nerves is temporarily affected, and the diaphragm tenses, or goes into a spasm. This is commonly called "winding".

The benefits of breath control

The diaphragm may be consciously moved and so we are able to control our breathing. Breathing exercises can improve health and fitness, and help to relieve tension.

- **Singing and acting** Breath control is the basis of these skills. It enables someone to create the right sound, at the right volume.
- **Stress relief** Controlled breathing clears lungs of waste, increases oxygen intake, improves posture and relaxes muscles.
- **Exercise** Athletes breathe deeply *before* exercising to flush carbon dioxide from the system and stimulate the production of energy.
- **Yoga** Breathing exercises relax the mind and body and help to maintain yoga positions.

△ This jazz trumpeter in New Orleans uses his diaphragm to control his breathing. All singers and wind-instrument players are trained to use the diaphragm in this way.

The chest

The chest is given its shape by the rib cage, which is made up of 12 pairs of ribs. Ribs are flat bones, hinged at the spine, that curve round to the front of the chest. The **sternum**, or breastbone, is a long, flat bone at the front of the body. The ribs are connected to the sternum by a flexible joint of cartilage.

The lower ribs are not directly connected to the sternum, but are attached by cartilage to the ribs above them. The bottom two ribs hang free and are known as "floating ribs".

▷ The rib cage protects the organs in the chest cavity. All of the ribs are joined to the spine at the back, and most of them are attached to the sternum by a joint made of cartilage.

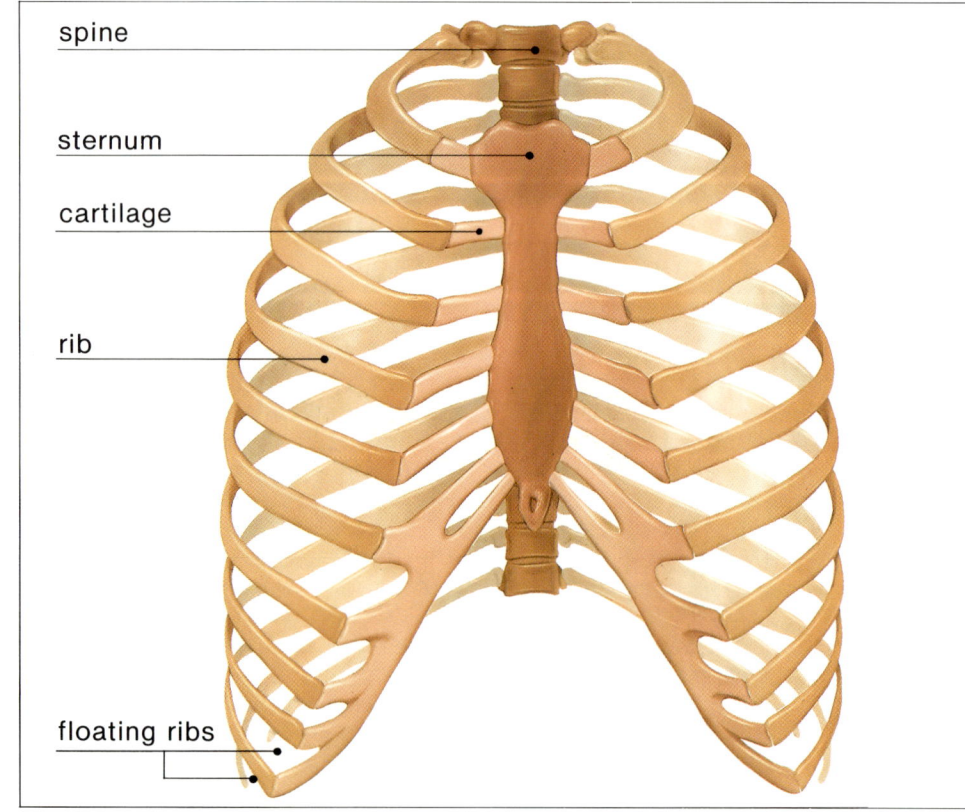

spine

sternum

cartilage

rib

floating ribs

This structure produces a rib cage that is immensely strong. At the same time, this cage is capable of movement. Unlike most other bones, ribs are very flexible and springy.

All the ribs are joined to the spine at the back of the body, and nearly all are attached to the sternum in front, or to each other in such a way that they can all be moved together, as the sternum is raised up and outward.

Between each set of ribs run two sheets of **intercostal muscles** which, as they contract, pull each rib closer to the next. This has the effect of raising the whole rib cage and increasing its volume.

As the muscles relax, the rib cage drops back down to its normal position and regains its original volume.

▽ The muscles running between the ribs can contract, or shorten. This lifts up the rib cage, increasing its volume, and giving the lungs more room to expand. When the intercostal muscles relax, the rib cage returns to its normal shape.

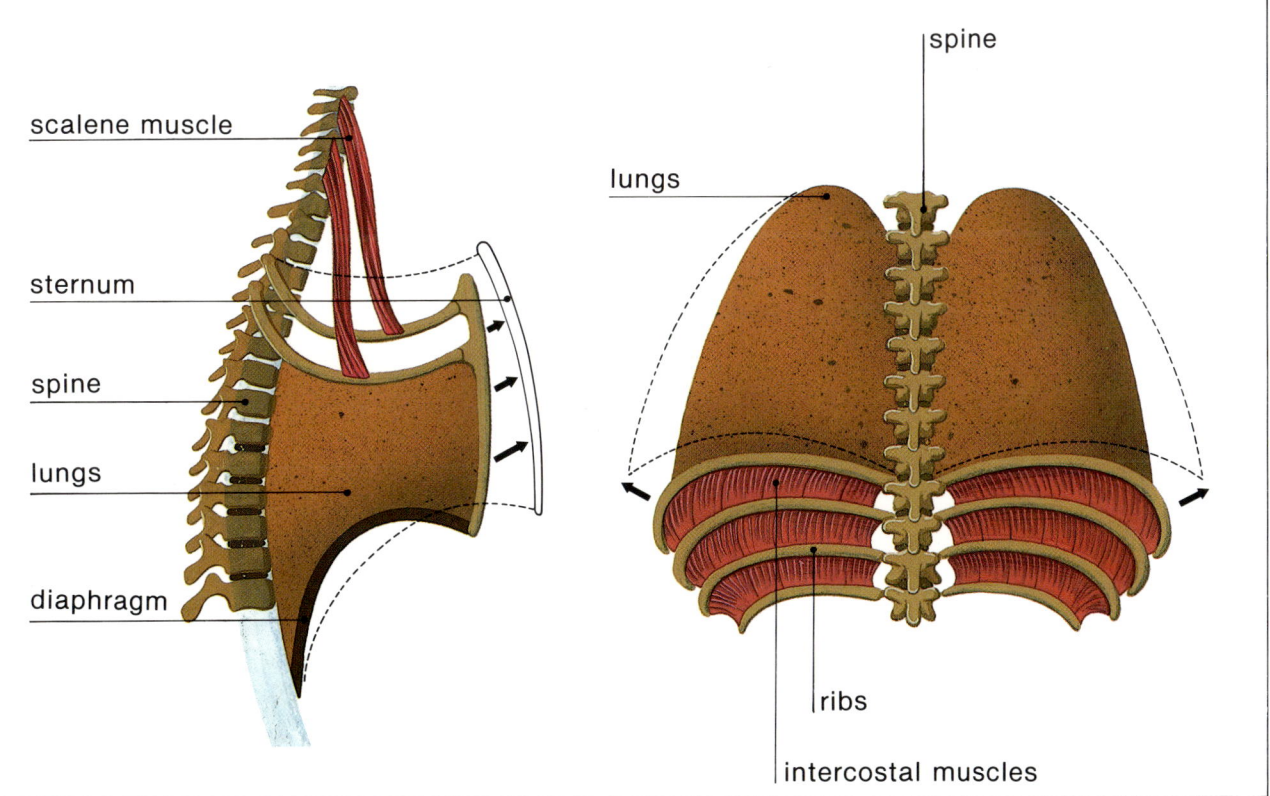

scalene muscle

sternum

spine

lungs

diaphragm

spine

lungs

ribs

intercostal muscles

How we breathe

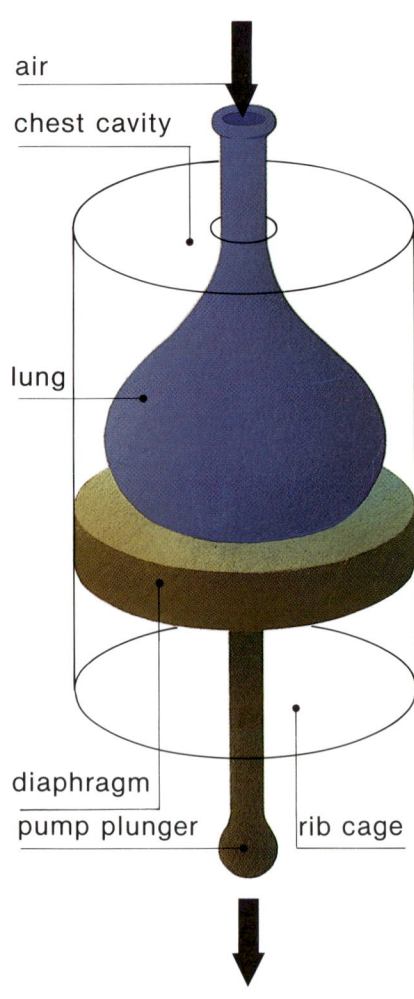

air

chest cavity

lung

diaphragm

pump plunger   rib cage

△ The lungs work like an air pump, the diaphragm acting as the plunger and the rib cage acting as the outer casing. When the diaphragm moves downwards, a vacuum is created, into which air rushes.

Normal quiet breathing is carried out by movement of the diaphragm. As it contracts, the diaphragm flattens out, increasing the volume of the chest cavity. Air rushes into the lungs to fill this extra space. In quiet breathing, the diaphragm moves down only about 1.5 cm (⅝ in), but in deep breathing it may move as much as 7.5 cm (3 in).

Breathing works like a bellows, or a water pump. We rely on the pressure of the air around us to push air through the airways and into the lungs as the volume of the chest cavity increases.

When the diaphragm relaxes, it regains its former dome shape, and the lungs are squeezed slightly, forcing the remaining air out again. We never completely empty our lungs. Even after breathing out as hard as possible, about 1.5 l (about 2½ pints) of air remain in the lungs.

This quiet diaphragmic breathing is the usual method of breathing, when the chest can hardly be seen to rise and fall. However, the abdomen can be seen moving gently as the diaphragm contracts and relaxes, pushing down on the organs below it.

When we exert ourselves, the muscles need a greater supply of oxygen from the blood, and the action of the diaphragm alone cannot provide deep enough breathing. The ribs are now used, being moved by the intercostal muscles to produce a much larger expansion and contraction of the chest, and with it, the lungs.

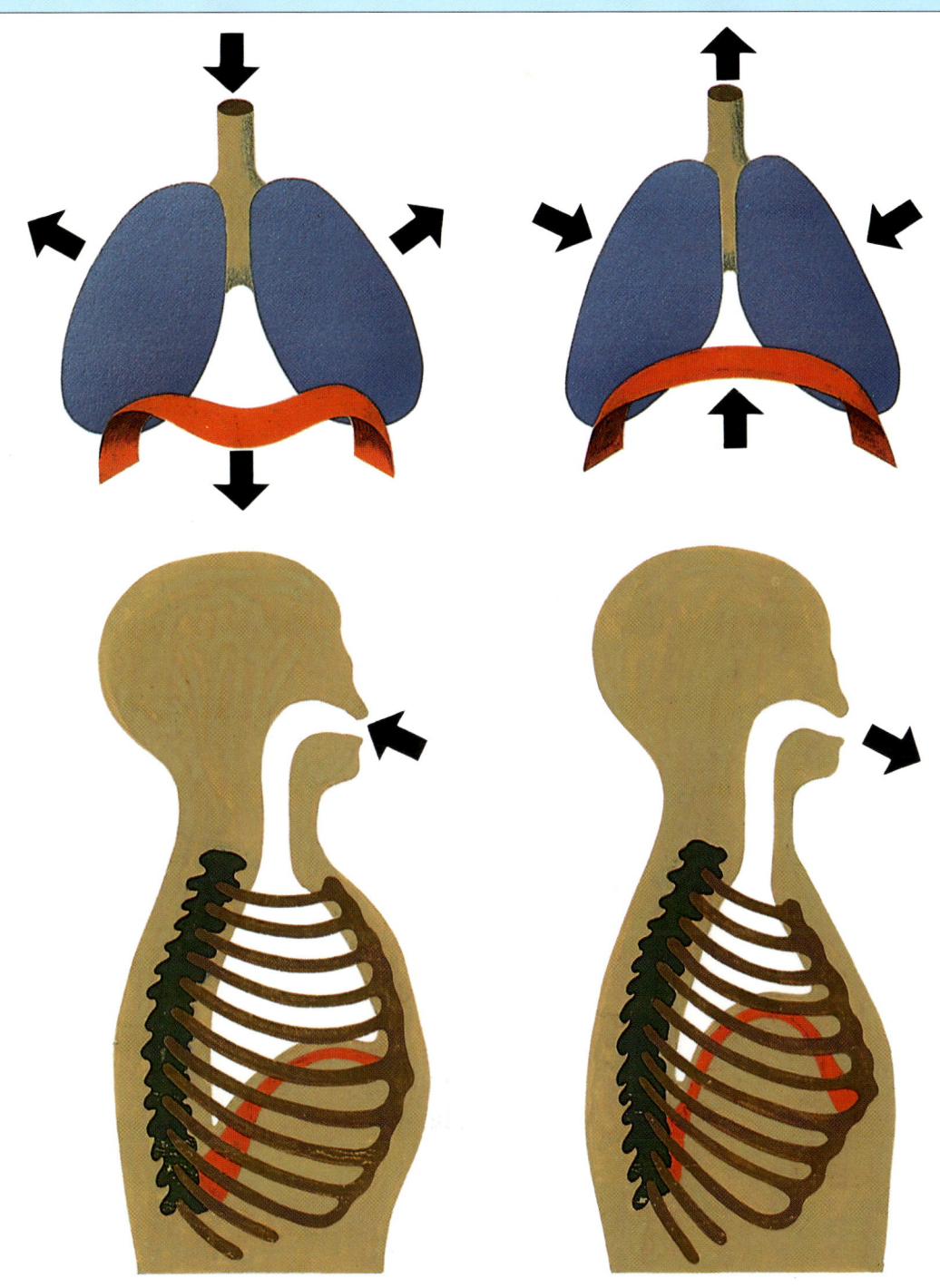

△ When we breathe in deeply, the diaphragm flattens and the intercostal muscles raise the rib cage. The volume of the rib cage increases and air rushes into the lungs.

△ When we breathe out, the diaphragm and intercostal muscles relax, and the rib cage decreases in volume. This forces the air out of the lungs through the nose or mouth.

What makes us breathe?

Breathing is completely automatic. It continues through consciousness and sleep without our having to make any active breathing effort. We can vary the rate of breathing, as usually happens when we stop to think about it, and we can consciously breathe more deeply.

What we cannot do is to stop breathing altogether for much more than about a minute. If the breath is held for long enough, automatic mechanisms in the body take over, and it becomes impossible to avoid taking a deep breath.

▽ Our rate of breathing is controlled by an extremely complex mechanism. The brain monitors messages it receives about the body's need for oxygen and the presence of waste carbon dioxide. It then instructs the respiratory system to make the necessary changes.

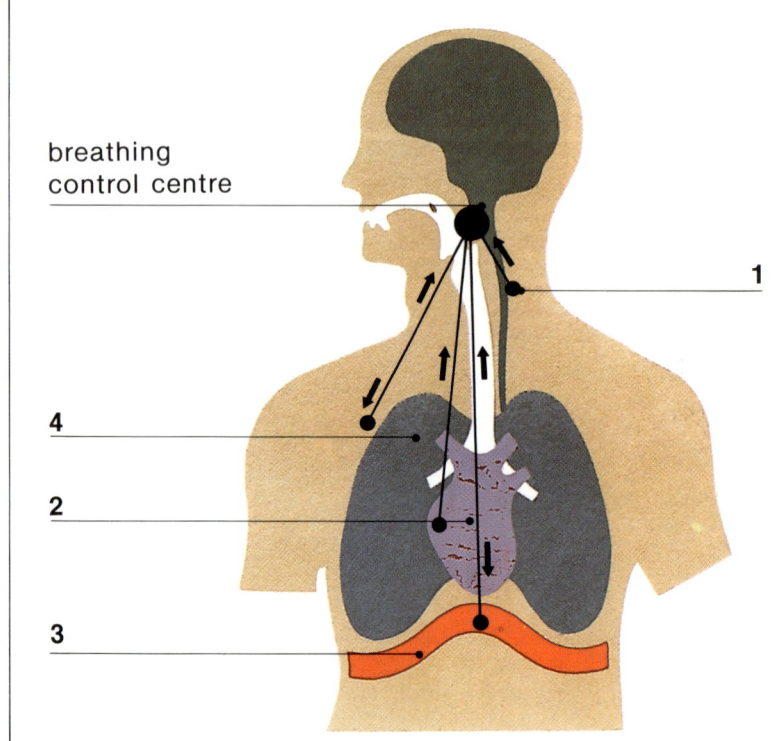

breathing control centre

1

4

2

3

● The breathing control centre measures the level of carbon dioxide in the blood and receives information from the intercostal muscles, diaphragm and stretch receptors in the lungs themselves.
1 The carotid body measures oxygen levels in the blood.
2 The level of carbon dioxide in the blood is also monitored.
3 Nerve signals are also passed to the diaphragm.
4 Instructions are also sent to the intercostal muscles of the rib cage.

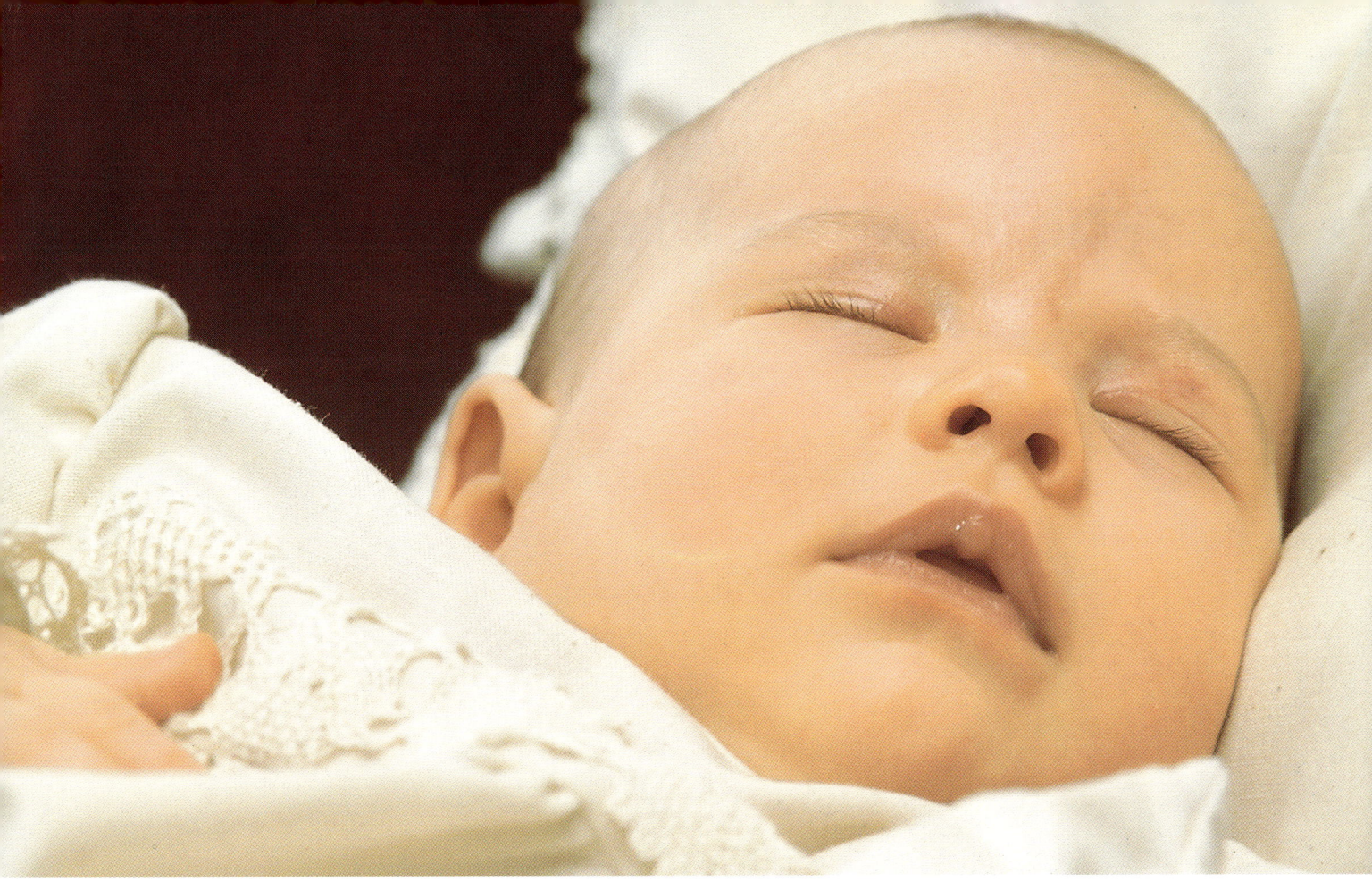

A part of the brain which controls all our body functions automatically sends nerve impulses down the spinal cord to the diaphragm and the intercostal muscles, instructing them to contract regularly.

The rate and depth of breathing is also controlled chemically. During exertion, muscles increase their production of waste carbon dioxide, which begins to build up in the blood. The control centre in the brain detects this increase in carbon dioxide and steps up the rate and depth of breathing to flush out the unwanted dissolved gas through the lungs.

Yet another mechanism measures the oxygen level of the blood through a chemical detector in a neck artery. This passes instructions to the brain to speed up the rate of breathing when oxygen is in short supply.

△ Breathing is an involuntary mechanism, regulated by the brain. When we are asleep, our bodies need less oxygen. The brain reduces breathing so that it is more shallow and slower than when we are awake.

Oxygen in the lungs

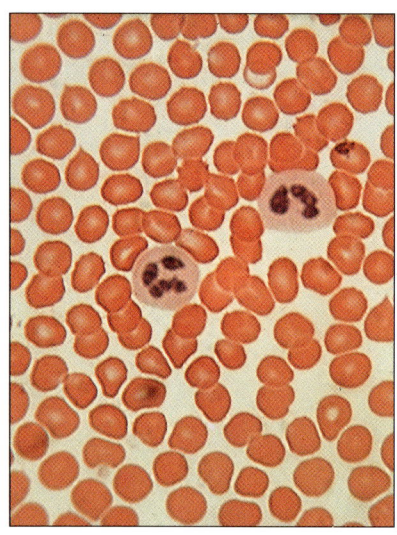

△ Red blood cells carry oxygen in the form of oxyhaemoglobin to all parts of the body. Here, a white cell, important in the immune system, is seen in the middle of a group of red blood cells.

At the ends of the smallest bronchioles are clusters of tiny air sacs called alveoli, in which oxygen is absorbed and carbon dioxide is released. There are more than 300 million alveoli in an adult's lungs, and together they have a huge surface area of 80 sq m (95 sq yd), or more than 40 times the whole surface area of the skin.

Alveoli have thin walls, only one cell thick, and they contain a network of fine **capillaries** that carry blood. Air that is rich in oxygen and contains little carbon dioxide enters the alveoli. The oxygen passes freely through the walls of the alveoli and the capillaries and enters the red blood cells. There the oxygen combines loosely with a red substance called **haemoglobin**, to form **oxyhaemoglobin**. The red cells move on in the bloodstream, now carrying oxygen to be given up to other body cells as needed.

Carbon monoxide, a gas found in tobacco smoke and vehicle exhaust, is also able to combine with haemoglobin and can stop the haemoglobin picking up oxygen. This causes breathlessness and worsens conditions like **asthma**.

Dissolved in the clear blood **plasma** in which red cells float is the waste gas carbon dioxide, produced by all the cells of the body. This passes out into the alveoli, and is flushed out of the lungs when we breathe out. Excess water is also produced by some chemical reactions in the body, and this evaporates into the air leaving the lungs.

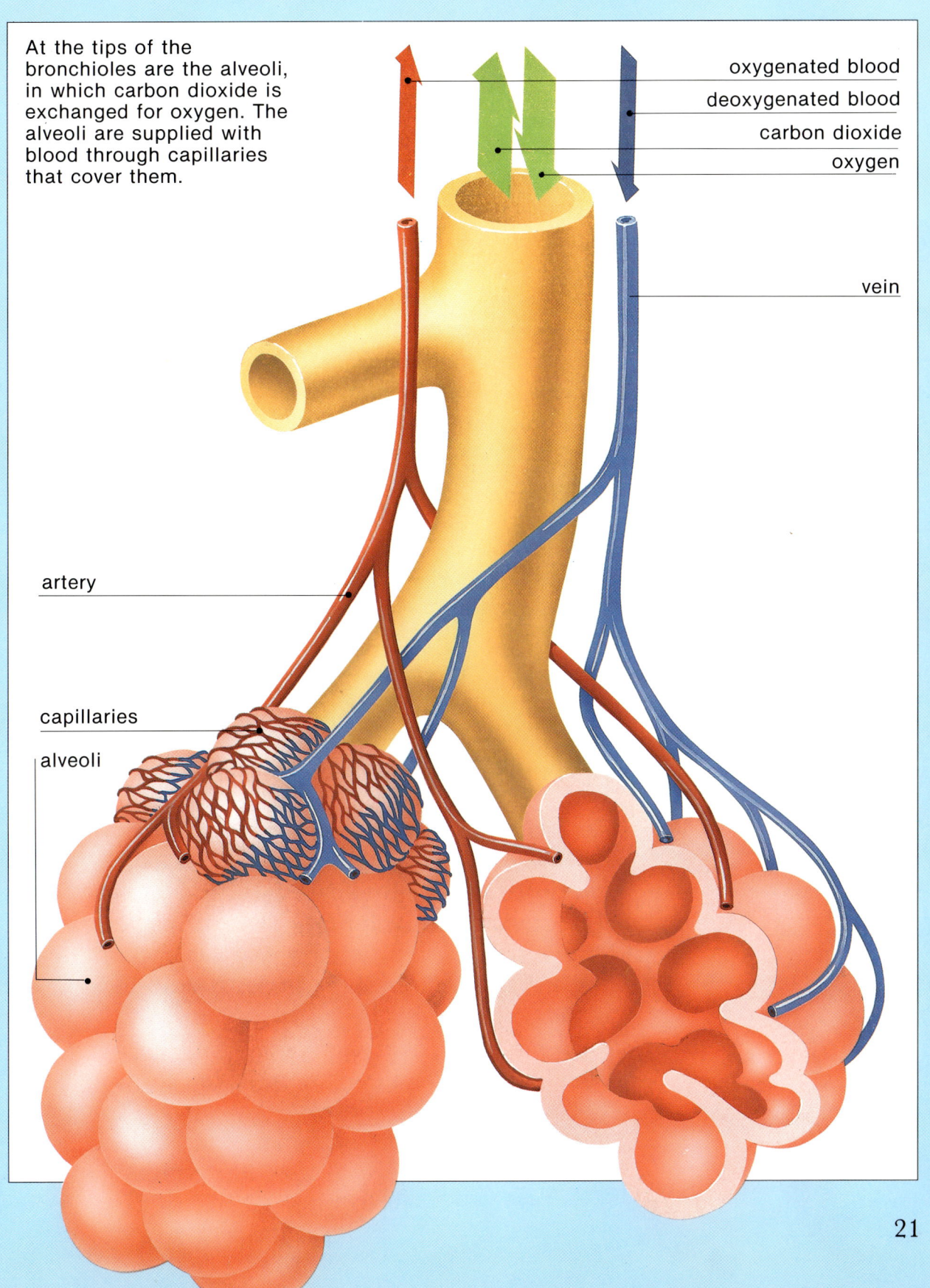

At the tips of the bronchioles are the alveoli, in which carbon dioxide is exchanged for oxygen. The alveoli are supplied with blood through capillaries that cover them.

oxygenated blood

deoxygenated blood

carbon dioxide

oxygen

vein

artery

capillaries

alveoli

Blood circulation to the lungs

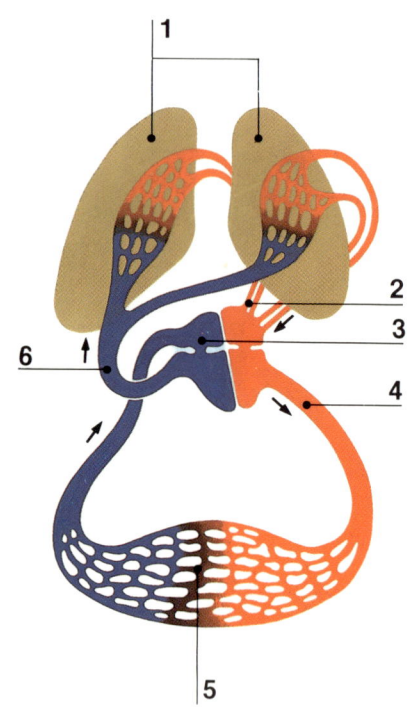

△ This diagram shows how the blood circulates around the body. The heart pumps deoxygenated blood (shown in blue) to the lungs to pick up oxygen and deposit its waste carbon dioxide. Oxygenated blood (shown in red) is then pumped to the rest of the body.

1 Lungs
2 Pulmonary veins
3 Heart
4 Aorta
5 Body circulation
6 Pulmonary artery

It would be wasteful if oxygenated blood were to become mixed with blood from which oxygen had already been used by the body and which contained waste carbon dioxide. To avoid this situation, blood is circulated in two stages.

The heart itself is divided into two parts, each pumping blood to a different part of the body. The left side of the heart is the more powerful, pumping oxygenated blood all around the body, through a huge network of arteries and capillaries.

As the blood passes through the capillaries, it gives up its oxygen to the cells, which use it to produce energy for all the body's activities. The blood takes in carbon dioxide and water. Now it is deoxygenated blood, which returns along veins to the right side of the heart.

Passing through the smaller, right side of the heart, blood is pumped directly to the lungs, through the **pulmonary artery** and then through capillaries in the lungs, where it picks up oxygen and loses its dissolved carbon dioxide and water. The oxygenated blood now returns to the left side of the heart. It is then pumped out through the aorta and around the body, repeating the cycle again.

In this way oxygenated and deoxygenated blood are kept quite separate in the circulation. Fresh oxygen is continually brought in through the lungs, and waste carbon dioxide and water are eliminated as fast as they are produced.

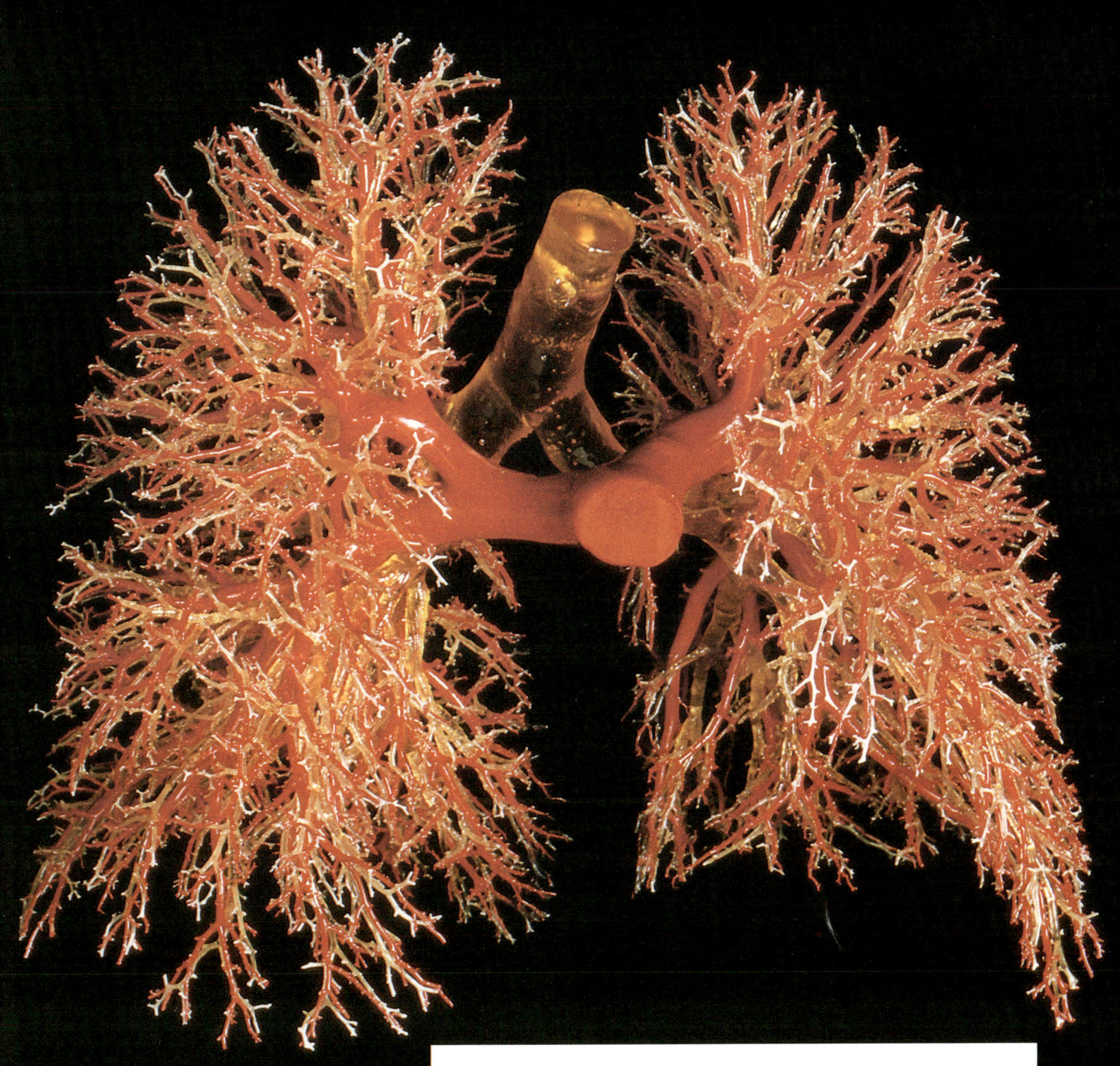

△ This model shows the arteries and bronchi that supply blood and air to the lungs. At the back of the model is the trachea (yellow), branching into the two bronchi and into the smaller bronchioles. In the centre is the pulmonary artery (red), which carries blood to the lungs to pick up oxygen.

Gas transfer in the tissues

△ This woman is using a Wright peak flow meter to measure the maximum flow of air she can breathe out. The test is used to check the efficiency of her lungs and so gauge her fitness.

Capillaries containing oxygenated blood penetrate almost every part of the body. The only living cells that do not have a blood supply are in parts of the eye, where blood would block vision. These cells must absorb their oxygen directly from the surrounding tissues.

All other cells are supplied with the oxygen carried in the red blood cells as oxyhaemoglobin, a bright red pigment.

Capillaries are never very far away from living cells, branching and twining through muscles, nerves and all other types of tissue. Oxygen splits off from the oxyhaemoglobin and enters the cells. Here it reacts with chemicals already in the cell to produce energy, which may be used by the cells or stored as a reserve power supply for later use. The same reaction produces carbon dioxide and water as waste products, which pass out of the cell into the blood.

The blood continues on its way, carrying dissolved carbon dioxide and additional water, the red cells now containing only haemoglobin (which is dark purplish-red).

This chemical process of the exchange of oxygen for carbon dioxide and water in the cell is called **respiration**.

Parts of the body having a high energy requirement need a greater blood supply. For this reason the brain and muscles all have very large blood supplies, and are penetrated by large numbers of capillaries.

Respiration and exercise

There are two forms of respiration: aerobic (with oxygen) and anaerobic (without oxygen).

● Aerobic respiration produces energy in cells using oxygen from red blood cells. Aerobic exercise includes swimming, cycling and jogging, which improve the efficiency of the lungs.

● Anaerobic respiration occurs during short bursts of activity like sprinting, when the body uses up so much oxygen that it cannot replace it quickly enough. The muscles must work without oxygen. Anaerobic respiration produces a waste product called lactic acid, which can only be broken down by oxygen.

▽ Capillaries carry oxygen in the form of oxyhaemoglobin from the lungs to all parts of the body. They also remove waste carbon dioxide. Areas of the body which require a lot of oxygen, such as muscles and the brain, contain large numbers of capillaries.

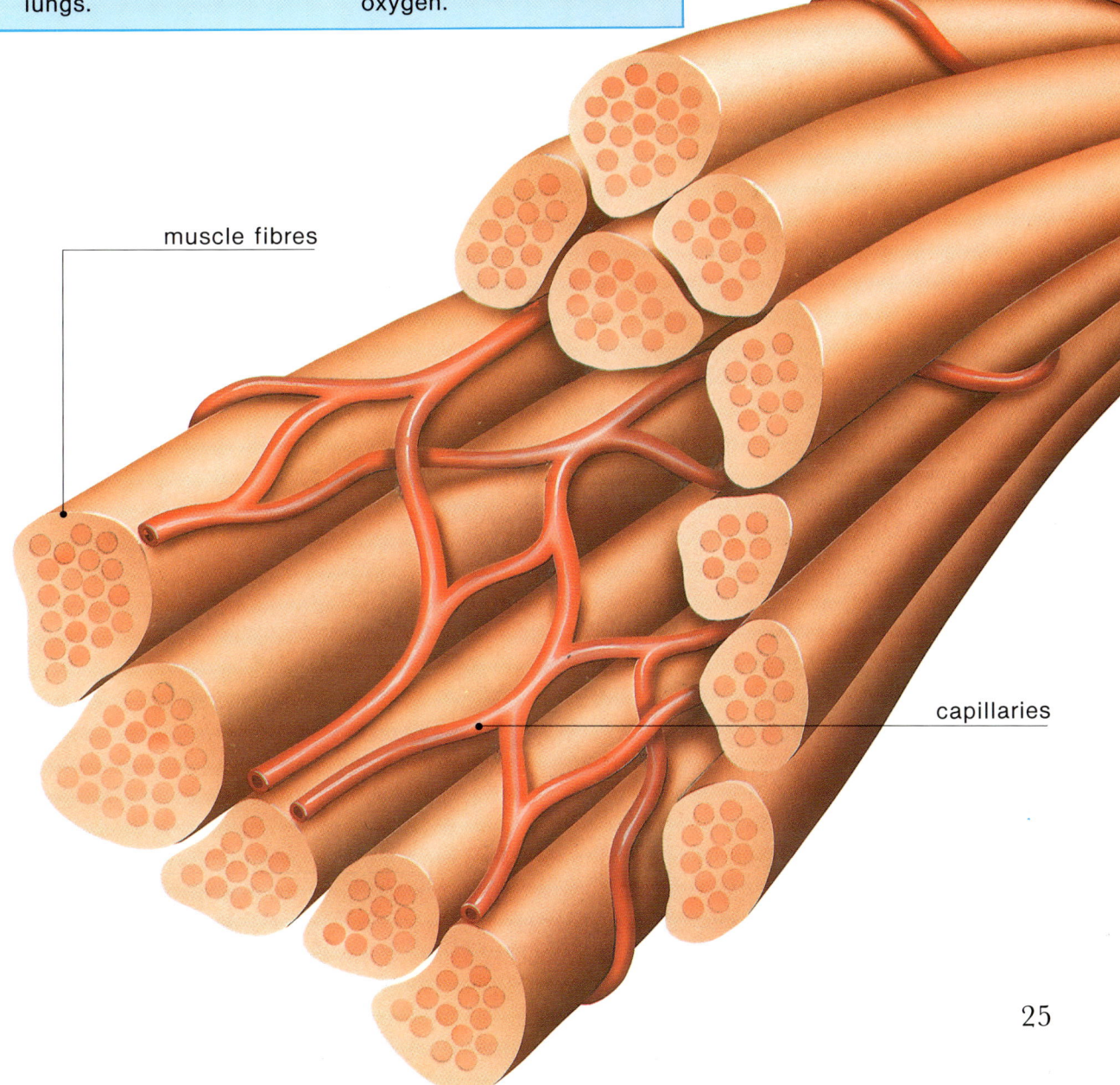

muscle fibres

capillaries

25

Cleaning the airways

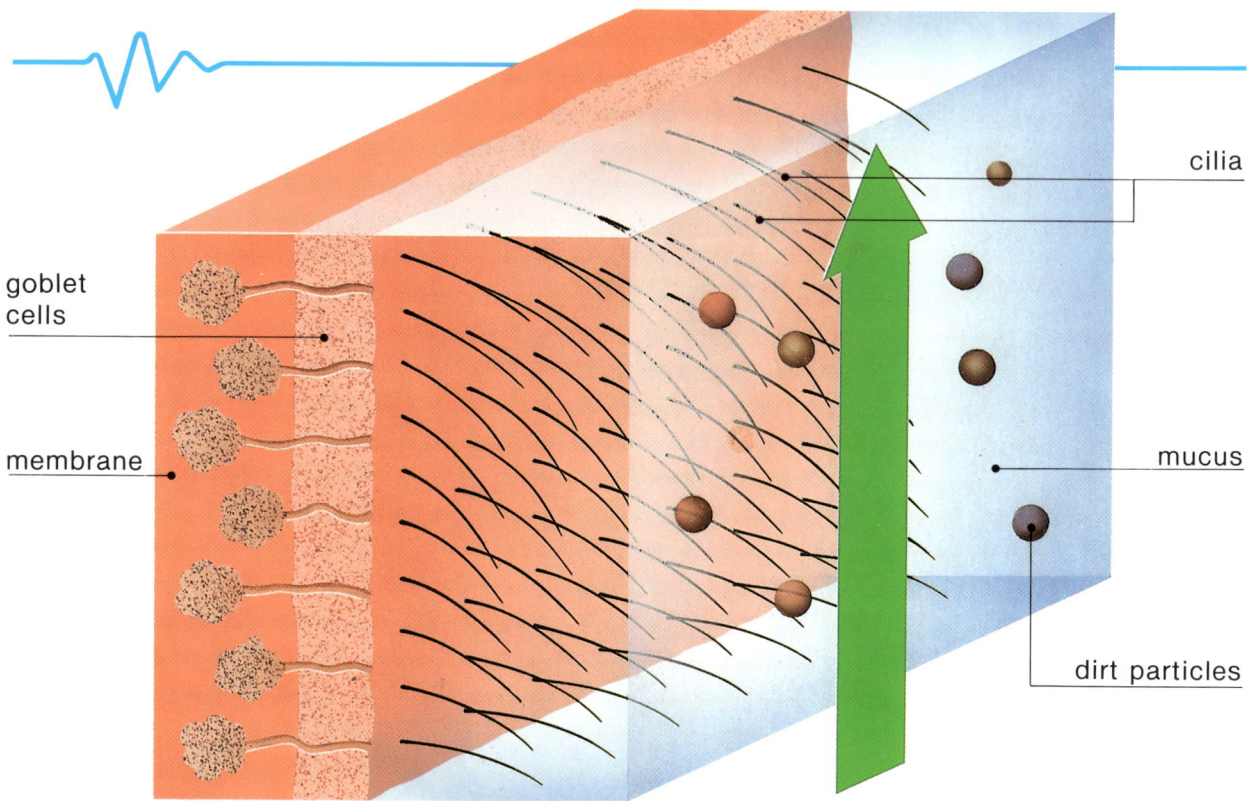

goblet
cells

membrane

cilia

mucus

dirt particles

△ This diagram shows the cilia, small hair-like structures, about to beat in the direction of the arrow. By doing so, they propel mucus out of the lungs, along with the dirt it has collected. The cilia are very delicate, and deposits of tar from smoking paralyzes them. This stops this essential cleaning mechanism and can lead to disease.

Even the cleanest air contains dirt particles, and these are deposited on the moist lining of the trachea, bronchi and bronchioles. There are special mechanisms to clean the lungs of most of this dirt.

The mucous membrane lining the trachea, bronchi and bronchioles is covered with cilia, which are tiny hair-like structures. Cilia beat back and forth, working together so that their movement is like that of wheat when gusts of wind blow across a field. Their rowing movement produces a current in the layer of sticky mucus, carrying it steadily towards the trachea together with most of the dirt particles. Dirt trapped in the mucus is moved out of the lungs at a rate of 1 cm (⅜ in) per minute.

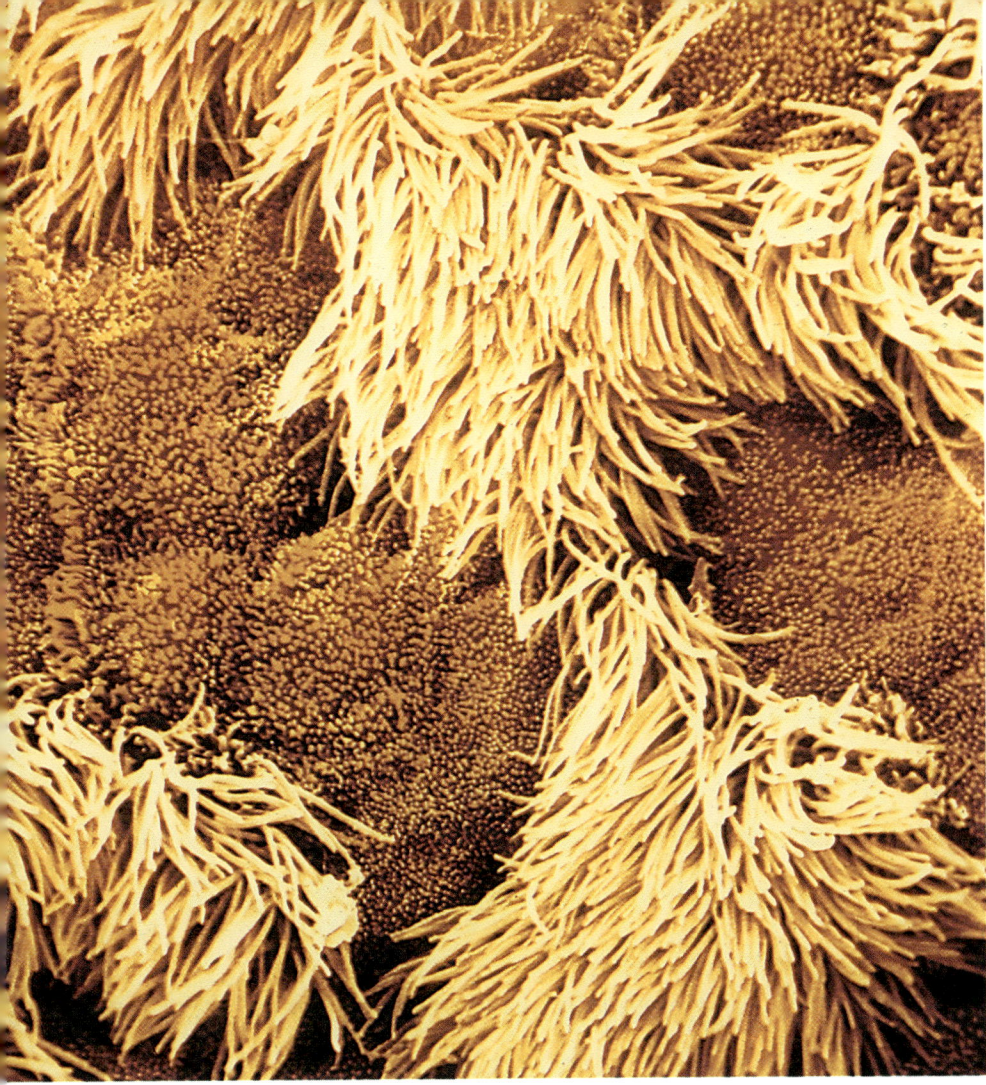

◁ This coloured microscope picture shows the tiny cilia in the trachea, looking like yellow grass. The cilia are interspersed with goblet cells that produce mucus.

Pollution

Air pollution includes:
- **Carbon monoxide**, mainly from vehicle exhaust and cigarette smoke
- **Sulphur oxides**, from burning coal and oil
- **Nitrogen oxides**, from power stations and vehicle exhaust
- **Particles of inorganic matter**, from industrial processes
- **Organic dust**, mostly pollen
- **Bacteria**, spread by air-conditioning systems

Pollution may cause serious diseases such as:
- **Bronchitis**, as a result of damage by tobacco smoke and airborne chemicals in urban areas
- **Lung cancer**, caused by tobacco smoke
- **Silicosis**, from silicon particles in the air found in all mines
- **Asbestosis**, from particles of asbestos used in some buildings to prevent fires spreading
- **Legionnaire's disease**, from bacteria in air-conditioning systems and water supplies
- **Farmer's lung**, caused by a bacterium in dust from mouldy hay

When it reaches the throat, it is swallowed and disposed of harmlessly.

Tobacco smoke has a direct effect on this system. It paralyzes the tiny beating cilia, allowing harmful tar to accumulate in the lungs. The tar remains in contact with living cells, rather than being removed quickly by the cilia, as with normal dirt particles. If a person stops smoking altogether, however, the cilia begin to work again, and the lungs are gradually cleaned of tar and other substances.

There are no cilia in the alveoli, and there a different protective mechanism is used. Dirt particles reaching the alveoli are enveloped by large white cells called **macrophages**. These can consume dirt and bacteria, preventing infection.

Coughing and sneezing

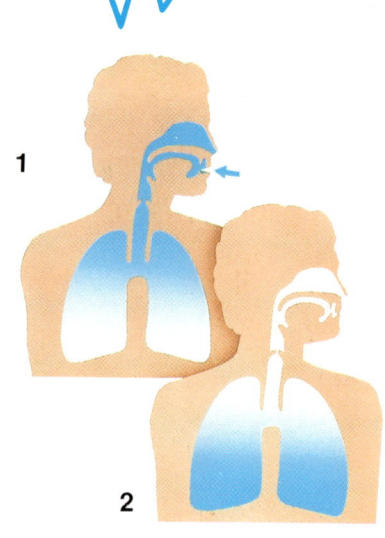

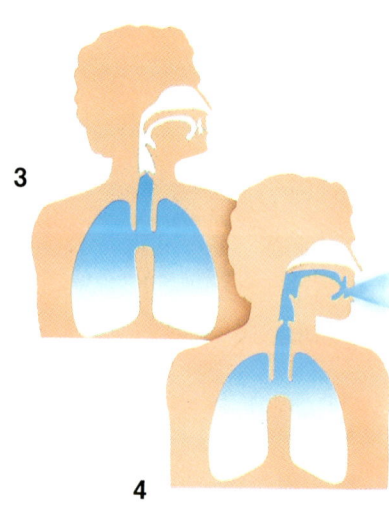

△ Irritation of the airways
causes us to cough.
1 A deep breath is inhaled.
2 The vocal cords close, to
seal off the airways
3 Intercostal muscles and
diaphragm contract,
compressing the air in the
lungs.
4 The vocal cords relax and
the air is expelled with force
through the mouth.

Some of the ways in which the respiratory
system clears itself of blockage or irritation are
very obvious. Any attempt by food or other
material to enter the air passages is met by an
explosive reaction of coughing, which is quite
uncontrollable.

In a cough, the diaphragm and rib muscles
contract violently. The **vocal cords** close for a
moment, as pressure builds up, and then release
the trapped air with a rush. The air travels out of
the trachea at as fast as 160 m (525 ft) per
second, usually dislodging the obstruction.

In a sneeze, the same explosive expulsion of air
takes place, but the soft palate blocks the back of
the nasal cavity. When the soft palate is suddenly
relaxed, air shoots out through the nose. When
we sneeze, air can travel at speeds of about 160
km (about 100 miles) per hour, and can
contain as many as 100,000 droplets of mucus
and germs.

Hiccups are a disorder of the breathing
apparatus, when for no obvious reason the
diaphragm contracts sharply. Instead of inhaling
in the normal way, the vocal cords slam shut,
producing the "hic" sound. Hiccups seem to
result from an incorrect message being passed
along the nerves to the diaphragm.

Laughing and crying both result from short,
sharp expulsions of breath, whereas yawning is
caused by a deep intake of breath, with the
mouth wide open.

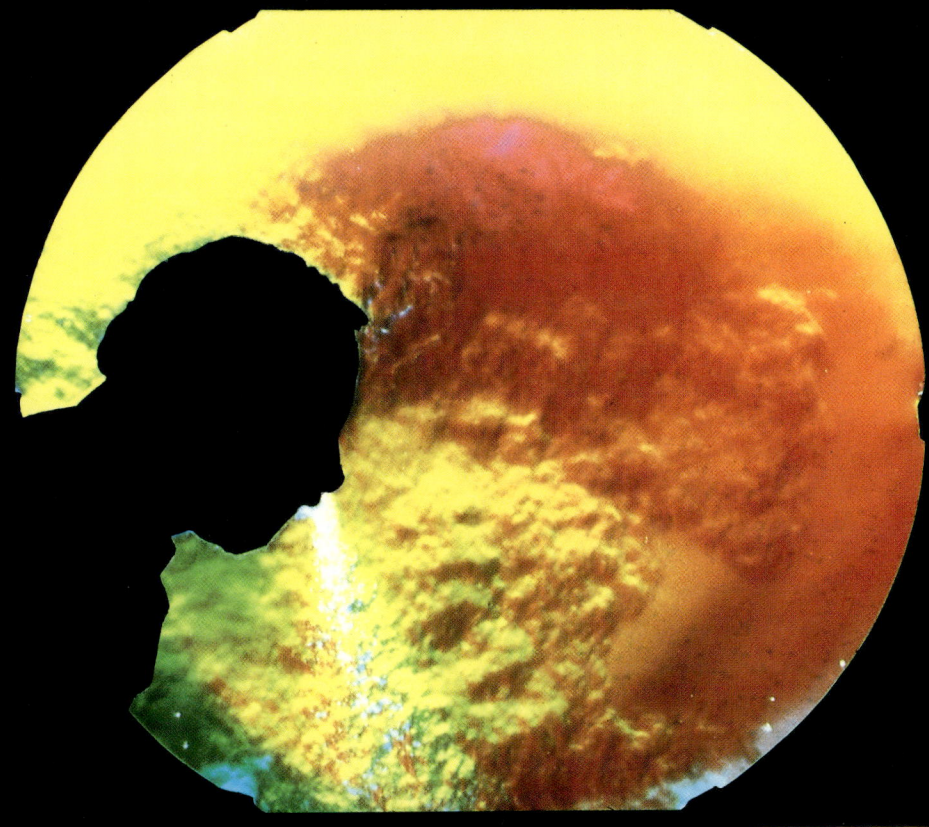

◁ A special photographic
process enables us to see
what happens when we
sneeze. Here, the man
sneezes and millions of tiny
droplets enter the air at high
speed, spreading his germs
to other people.

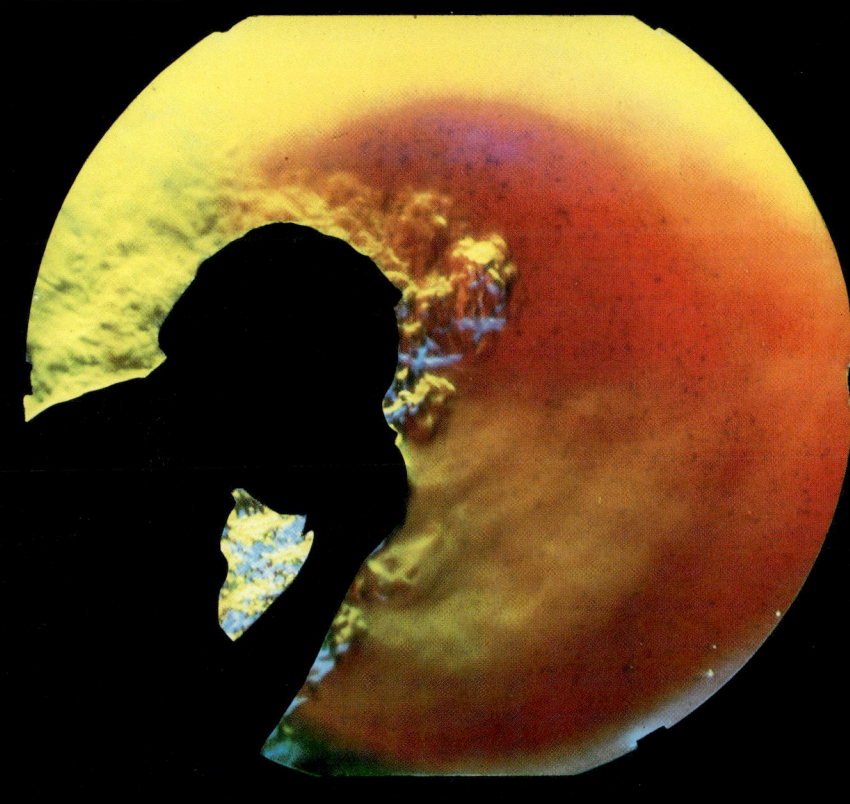

▷ In this photograph, the
man is sneezing into a
handkerchief. He is able to
catch many of the droplets
and so helps to prevent the
spread of diseases such as
colds and influenza.

Smoking and health

Harming others

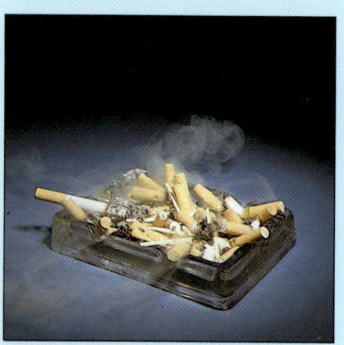

People who smoke damage their own health, but they also expose non-smokers to the harmful effects of cigarette smoke.

- Involuntary or passive smoking can cause disease, including lung cancer, in healthy non-smokers.
- The children of parents who smoke have a greater risk of breathing problems and lung infections.
- A woman who smokes during pregnancy has a very much greater chance of giving birth to a premature or unhealthy baby.

Smoking tobacco is an addictive habit. There are many reasons why people start smoking, from simple curiosity to the desire to seem grown-up. The addictive chemical in tobacco is **nicotine**, an extremely powerful drug.

Cigarette smoke contains carbon monoxide, tar and other poisonous chemicals as well as nicotine, and these have a harmful effect on all parts of the body. The lungs are especially vulnerable. They can be affected by lung cancer and other diseases, including bronchitis and **emphysema**.

Smoking affects the heart, by making it beat faster. Carbon monoxide takes the place of oxygen in the blood and so it takes more effort to provide enough oxygen for the cells. Smoking also affects the intestines, bladder, stomach and reproductive system.

The mouth and throat may develop cancer, and the teeth become yellow and unsightly. Headaches are common and frequent among smokers, and a narrowing of the blood vessels in the brain may lead to strokes.

If a woman smokes while she is pregnant, she may harm her baby. During pregnancy, the baby relies on its mother's blood to provide it with oxygen. If the mother continues to smoke, her blood is contaminated with poisons which are many times more lethal to the delicate baby than to the mother. The baby may be born prematurely and underweight or it may even be stillborn.

▷ The lungs of a newborn
baby are pink in colour but,
as we grow older, our lungs
become slightly discoloured.
This cross-section through a
healthy human lung shows a
few deposits of dirt, which
is normal.

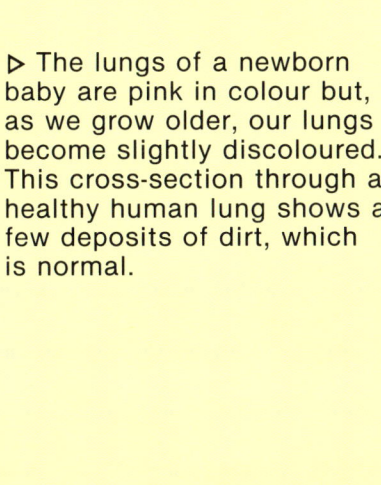

◁ This is a cross-section
through a smoker's lung. It
has tar, from smoking
cigarettes, deposited
throughout its structure and
shows signs of disease.

31

Giving up smoking

Since about the late 1960s, the number of people who smoke has decreased. Today, while overall the numbers of people smoking are still falling, the number of women taking up the habit is rising.

The pressure on smokers to give up or not smoke in the company of others has never been greater. Many buses, trains, cinemas, theatres, hospitals, shops and restaurants now ban smoking. Advertising cigarettes and tobaccos is now strictly controlled and is being replaced by anti-smoking campaigns.

There are several good ways of trying to give up the habit. You can simply stop and vow never to smoke again. For a while, the ex-smoker suffers withdrawal effects, a craving for nicotine, but this passes quite quickly. Another way is to start by reducing the number of cigarettes smoked and to switch to a low-tar brand. This does not remove the health risks of smoking and should be followed by stopping altogether after a short time.

"Flooding" is a method by which the smoker smokes as many cigarettes as possible, one after the other, until he or she feels sick and the desire to smoke is replaced by nausea at the smell of burning tobacco.

Other methods include group therapy, in which smokers and ex-smokers get together to help each other along the road to health. A doctor may prescribe aids such as nicotine chewing gum to help the smoker to kick the habit.

Anti-smoking campaigns are now being aimed at the young in an effort to reduce the numbers of people taking up a habit that could kill them.

Breathing problems

△ The bronchioles are surrounded by muscles. In asthma, these muscles contract, narrowing the airways and making it difficult to breathe.

The respiratory system can be affected by many illnesses, and is particularly prone to bacterial and **virus** infections, because it is in direct contact with germ-laden air.

The viruses of the common cold and influenza enter the body through the nasal passages and lungs, and leave the body the same way to spread the infection. Most common diseases also enter through the lungs but these do not usually cause such noticeable breathing problems. Tuberculosis is a lung infection caused by certain bacteria. This disease is now less common in countries with adequate health care.

One of the most common breathing problems is bronchitis, caused by inflammation of the bronchi by infection, smoking or some other condition. The bronchi become partly blocked by mucus, causing great difficulty in breathing. Emphysema also results in breathing problems, when large areas of the lungs cease to work properly, causing breathlessness.

Asthma is caused by contraction of the muscles wrapped around the bronchioles, narrowing them and restricting the flow of air. It is sometimes caused by an **allergy**, an over-reaction of the body's defences to harmless dust or pollen in the air. **Hay fever** is a common allergy which causes a runny nose, sneezing and watery eyes, usually because of a reaction to pollen. It is generally seasonal, depending on which types of pollen are in the air at a particular time of year.

△ Asthma in children often disappears during the teenage years. Sometimes, however, the condition recurs throughout life. To relieve their asthma, sufferers use an inhaler containing a drug that relaxes the muscles around the bronchioles.

Hay fever

Hay fever is caused by an allergic reaction to pollen from trees in spring and grass in summer. The medical name for hay fever is seasonal allergic rhinitis. It affects many people. In Great Britain alone, about 8 million people have been or will be affected by hay fever. Symptoms of hay fever are most likely to appear in the teenage years or in the early twenties, and many people stop suffering from the condition after about 10 years.

The symptoms of hay fever include irritation of the nose, sneezing attacks, watering eyes and a prickly throat.

The throat and voice

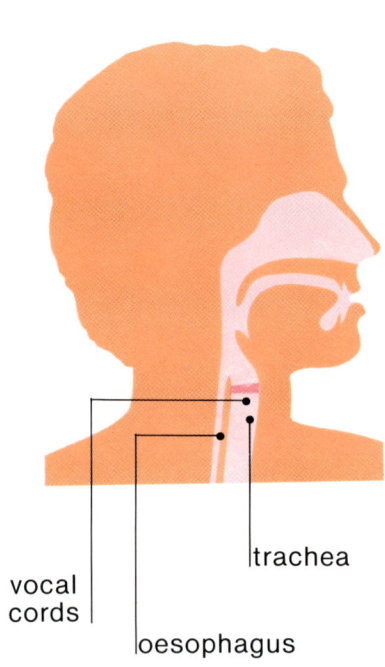

vocal cords

oesophagus

trachea

△ The larynx or "Adam's apple" contains the vocal cords. It is positioned at the top of the trachea, towards the front of the throat.

All the air entering the lungs passes through the **larynx**, or voice box. This is made up of tough cartilage and is positioned at the top of the trachea. In some people, you can see the larynx as the bulging "Adam's apple" in the front of the neck.

One important function of the larynx is the production of sound, and it contains the basic mechanism for the production of the human voice.

The larynx is a tubular box. Across its hollow centre are stretched two leathery sheets, the vocal cords, with a small triangular gap between them. Several muscles control the tension of the vocal cords. When the muscles contract, the cords are

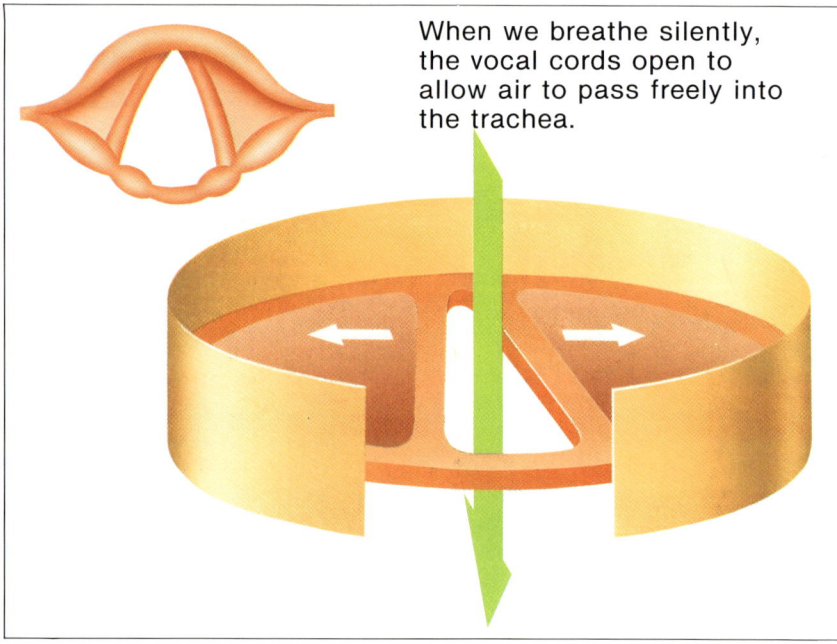

When we breathe silently, the vocal cords open to allow air to pass freely into the trachea.

brought closer, narrowing or closing the gap.

All the air we breathe passes between the vocal cords. When they are brought closer together, with only a slit between them, they vibrate in the rush of air, exactly like the reed in a clarinet or mouth organ. This generates sound.

We often use our vocal cords without thinking about it. We open them to allow air to pass freely into the lungs in normal, quiet breathing. When we want to talk, shout or sing, we use a combination of vocal cords, lungs, mouth and tongue to produce the sound we want.

The tighter the vocal cords are stretched, the higher the pitch of the sound produced becomes. Loudness depends on the amount of air being forced between them.

The quality of the sound produced is affected by resonance, or echoing, in the mouth, nasal cavity, sinuses and chest. This is why blocked sinuses or a cold cause the voice to sound muffled and distorted.

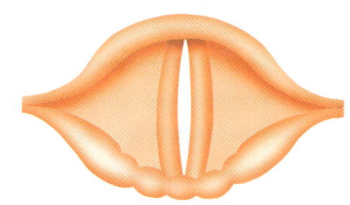

Sore throats

Most sore throats are caused by viruses or bacteria. They usually clear up after a few days.

- **Tonsillitis** Swelling of the tonsils (two glands that lie between the mouth and pharynx), caused by an infection. It may be treated with antibiotics.
  If tonsillitis persists, it may be necessary to have the tonsils removed.
- **Laryngitis** Inflammation of the larynx, sometimes leading to hoarseness and loss of voice. It is important to rest the voice.
- **Pharyngitis** Inflammation of the pharynx at the back of the mouth.

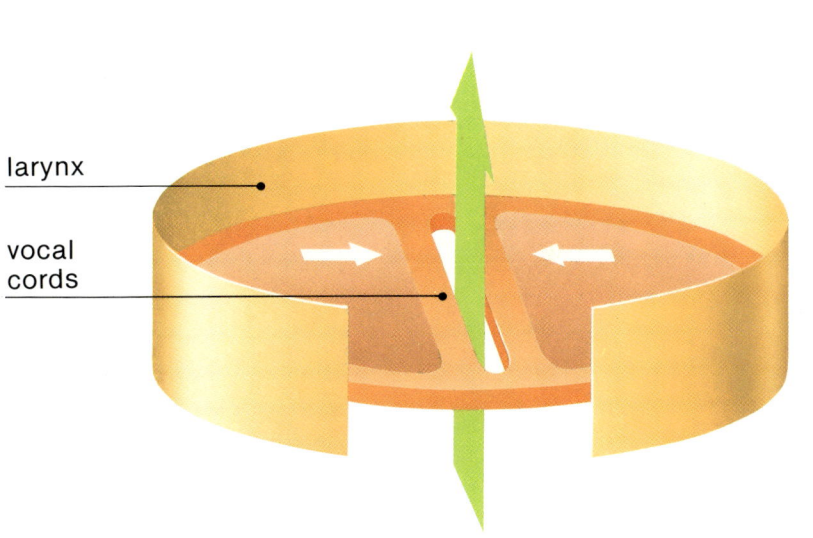

larynx

vocal cords

When we want to speak, the vocal cords draw closer, forming a small slit. Air is forced through this slit, causing the cords to vibrate, producing sound. The kinds of sounds we produce depend on the shape of the mouth and lips.

The human voice

The larynx can produce sound as air rushes between the vocal cords. But in order to form recognizable words, the sounds need to be altered and controlled, linked together and separated to make understandable speech. All this requires very complicated actions by many muscles, moving the jaw, tongue, lips, soft palate and cheeks, in addition to sound control in the larynx.

The teeth and the hard palate, the bony roof of the mouth, also play an important part in speech production or articulation.

Different combinations of actions are required to produce each group of sounds.

Stop sounds like "b" and "p" are produced by

▽ To produce the sound "mmm", the lips are closed and air is directed through the nose. The sound "ahh" is made when the mouth is open and air flows through freely.

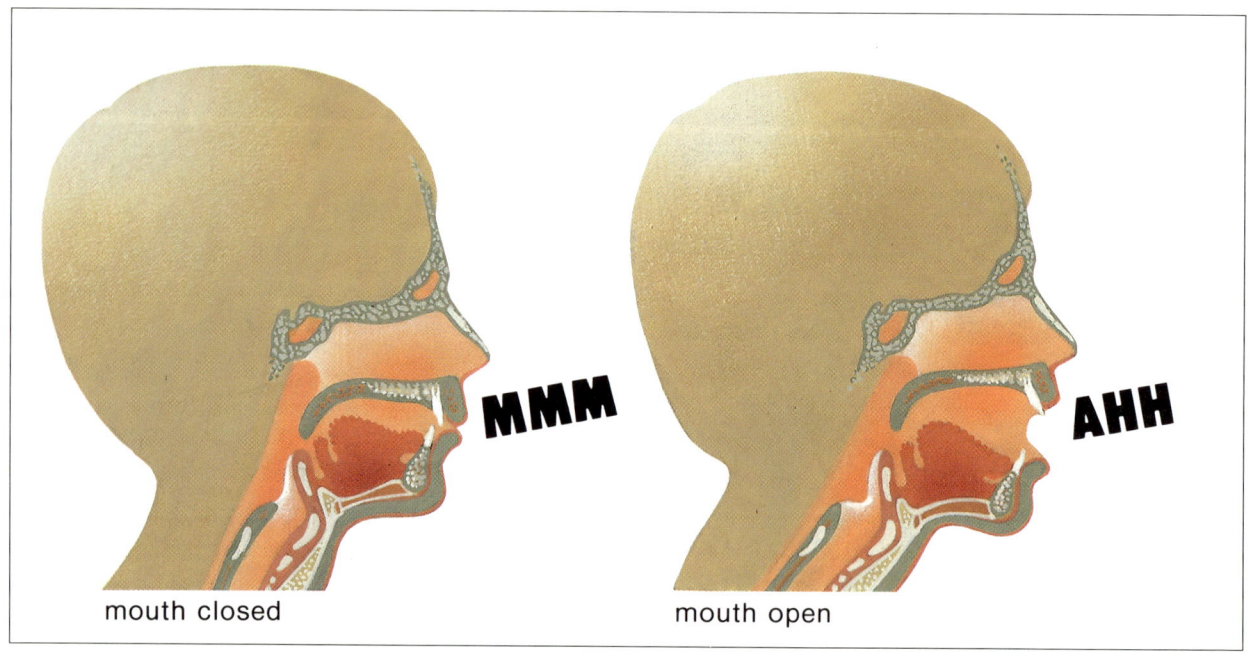

mouth closed

MMM

mouth open

AHH

suddenly blocking the flow of air with the lips. In "d" and "t", the flow of air is blocked by the tongue against the hard palate and the teeth; in "g" and "k" it is blocked against the soft palate.

Fricatives are sounds produced by partly blocking the air flow and forcing it through a narrow opening: "v", "f", "s" and "z" are all sounds of this type. To produce vowels, the quality of sound is varied by changing the position of the lips and jaw.

In sounds like "m", "n" and "ng", the air flow is directed through the nasal cavity, and the mouth is closed off.

Some sounds occur only in certain languages and dialects. Examples are the rolled "r" of the Scottish dialect and the guttural "ch" of German.

△ The human voice can be either very quiet or very loud and when a large number of people get together, the sound created can be very powerful indeed.

Swallowing

The opening into the larynx is at the back of the tongue. It is positioned in front of the gullet, or oesophagus. This means that air and food must at first share the same passage. A special mechanism is needed to prevent food from passing into the larynx and blocking the trachea, which would cause choking and suffocation.

Food in the mouth is first positioned by the tongue. As it passes back towards the throat, the soft palate is raised, blocking off the airway into the nasal cavity and preventing the food from entering it. The food is then forced into the throat, ready for swallowing.

▷ When we swallow, the larynx automatically prevents food entering the airways to the lungs.

The larynx is now raised against the base of the tongue and forced firmly against a small flap called the **epiglottis**, which seals off the airway into the larynx. You can feel this raising of the larynx in your neck: when you swallow, your "Adam's apple" rises.

Food can now pass directly into the oesophagus with no risk of being inhaled, and is carried down to the stomach by waves of muscular contraction called **peristalsis**.

If, because of hurried swallowing, food does lodge in the larynx, choking may follow, but the food is usually dislodged by coughing. When a very large piece of food is swallowed, you may feel as though you are choking, as the oesophagus bulges between the horseshoe-shaped cartilage rings causing the trachea to be partly blocked and temporarily interfering with the air flow to the lungs.

When we swallow, the soft palate closes off the entrance to the lungs.

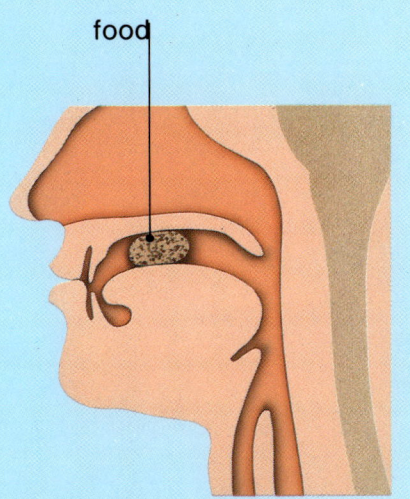

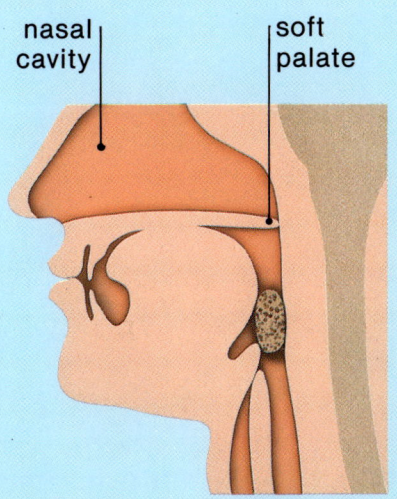

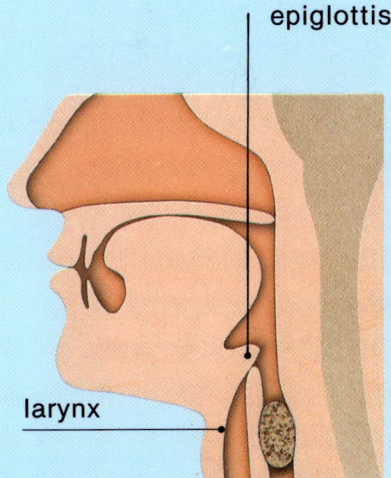

1 Food is chewed in the mouth and made into a ball, called a "bolus", which is easy to swallow.

2 The tongue positions the bolus, and as it leaves the mouth, the soft palate seals off the nasal cavity.

3 As the food is swallowed, the larynx rises, sealing off the airway against the epiglottis and preventing choking.

41

Aquatic man

Swimming does not always come naturally to us, but the human body is surprisingly well adapted to an aquatic existence. We can hold our breath for long enough to swim underwater for a minute or so. With practice, air can be kept out of the nose, simply by blocking off the airway through the nose with the soft palate. The pressure of the air already in the nasal cavity then prevents the entry of water.

We also possess an unusual mechanism that may be a throwback to aquatic ancestors. When the face is submerged in cold water, the body directs blood away from the skin and muscles, and increases the blood flow to the internal organs. In this way, the amount of oxygen used is reduced and heat loss to the water also decreases. Similar mechanisms exist in ducks, whales and other warm-blooded animals.

When we dive deeply, the water presses with great force on the body. A deep-sea diver breathes compressed air at the same pressure as the water outside, so the chest is not crushed, even though there may be many tons of water pressure on the body.

At these high pressures, nitrogen as well as oxygen is absorbed from the air through the lungs and dissolves in the bloodstream. If the diver surfaces too quickly after a long, deep dive, the nitrogen can form bubbles in the blood and cause a painful and serious condition called "the bends".

▷ This diver wears oxygen equipment to enable him to stay underwater for long periods of time. When divers are making very deep dives they must time their dives carefully and be aware of the depth at which they are swimming. If they are to avoid the bends, they must rise to the surface slowly, in easy stages.

Breathing at high altitudes

The higher you go above sea level, the thinner the air becomes, and there is less oxygen to breathe. In order to get sufficient oxygen, mountain climbers pant more as they reach greater heights. The summit of Mount Everest, rising to about 9,000 m (29,000 ft) above sea level, is just about the maximum altitude at which it is possible to survive for any length of time without extra oxygen. Even so, mountaineers usually wear oxygen equipment at such heights to avoid altitude sickness.

Aircraft now fly routinely at 10,000 m (33,000 ft) or more, where life would be impossible without artificial oxygen supplies. Modern airliners are pressurized so that the pressure inside their passenger cabins is equivalent to that at about 2,000 m (6,500 ft), which is hardly noticeable to the passengers.

In parts of Africa, Asia and South America, many people live permanently at high altitudes, and in the Andes some live as high as 5,000 m (16,500 ft) above sea level. We would find such life very uncomfortable, but in people born and living under these conditions, body changes have taken place which allow them to remain healthy. Their chests are enlarged to give them greater lung capacity, and their blood contains a much higher proportion of red cells than our own, so it can carry more oxygen. There are disadvantages too, because these barrel-chested South American Indians are very prone to lung disease.

▷ Mountaineers use artificial oxygen supplies to prevent altitude sickness. Here, Chris Bonington uses breathing apparatus as he stands on the summit of Mount Everest.

Altitude sickness

Altitude sickness occurs when the level of oxygen in the blood is reduced because of low atmospheric pressure at high levels. Most people are affected at about 4,000 m (14,000 ft).

Symptoms:
● coughing spasms
● headache and weakness
● irregular breathing
● loss of appetite
● loss of co-ordination
● nausea
● sleeplessness
● swelling of the fingers or face

Remedies:
The condition may be relieved by descending to a lower level, but it can kill. Even athletes have died from altitude sickness in places such as the Himalayas.

Glossary

Allergy: reaction by the body, usually caused by harmless substances, to which the person has become over-sensitive. May cause sneezing, watery eyes, rashes, etc.

Alveoli: tiny air sacs in the lungs in which oxygen is absorbed from the air and carbon dioxide is removed from the blood.

Aorta: the largest artery in the body, through which all the blood leaving the left side of the heart passes, to be pumped around the body.

Asthma: disease in which the small airways or bronchioles in the lungs become suddenly narrowed, obstructing the air flow. Asthma may be a form of allergy.

Bronchi: pair of airways branching off from the trachea, passing air to and from the right and left lungs.

Bronchioles: the smallest airways in the lungs, conveying air to the alveoli.

Bronchitis: disease in which the bronchi become inflamed and partly blocked by jelly-like mucus.

Capillaries: the smallest blood vessels. Capillaries penetrate virtually every part of the body, and are important in the exchange of oxygen and carbon dioxide in the lungs.

Carbon dioxide: (CO_2) colourless gas produced by the body as a waste product. CO_2 dissolves in the blood, and is removed in the lungs.

Carbon monoxide: (CO) colourless gas that is extremely poisonous. CO is found in cigarette smoke and motor vehicle exhaust.

Cartilage: whitish translucent material, which is slightly rubbery. Cartilage cushions joints and is also used to reinforce certain parts of the body.

Cell: smallest unit of the living body.

Cilia: hair-like structures in the mucous membrane that beat back and forth, producing a current in the mucus.

Diaphragm: tough sheet of muscle separating the organs of the chest from those in the abdomen. The diaphragm plays an important part in breathing.

Emphysema: lung disease in which the alveoli are damaged and no longer function properly, reducing the capacity of the lungs to absorb oxygen.

Epiglottis: small flap in the back of the throat that can close to block off the entrance to the larynx, preventing food from entering the airways.

Fricatives: sounds produced during speech, where the air flow through the mouth is partly blocked.

Goblet cells: cup-shaped cells lining the trachea and bronchi (also found elsewhere in the body), that produce sticky mucus.

Haemoglobin: dark red pigment carried in red blood cells. Oxygen becomes attached to haemoglobin and is transported to all parts of the body.

Hay fever: an allergy mostly affecting the eyes and nose. Pollen in the air causes an allergic reaction in which the nose itches, and the nose and eyes run continuously.

Intercostal muscles: sheets of muscles lying between the ribs, and used in deep breathing.

Larynx: the voice box or "Adam's apple". The larynx is made from cartilage, and is positioned on top of the trachea, at the front of the throat.

Ligament: tough, ropy material used to support joints and organs. Ligaments help hold the diaphragm in its relaxed, curved shape.

Lungs: paired spongy organs in the chest, through which oxygen is absorbed and carbon dioxide is removed from the blood.

Macrophages: large white cells that wander through the lungs, keeping them clean by consuming bacteria and particles of dirt.

Mucous membrane: thin, moist layer covering most of the organs of the body. Mucous membrane lines the trachea, bronchi and bronchioles.

Mucus: sticky liquid secreted from goblet cells in the mucous membrane, in which dirt particles become stuck and can be removed from the body. Mucus also acts as a protecting film and lubricant.

Nasal conchae: (or turbinates) thin ledges of bone in the nasal cavity that are covered in mucous membrane. These help to clean and warm incoming air.

Nicotine: poisonous drug found in cigarette smoke, which causes addiction.

Oesophagus: the gullet. Tube through which food is conveyed from the mouth to the stomach.

Oxygen: colourless gas present in the air, needed by every cell in the body. Oxygen is absorbed through the lungs into the blood.

Oxyhaemoglobin: substance formed when oxygen becomes attached to haemoglobin in the blood. Oxyhaemoglobin is bright red.

Palate: roof of the mouth, divided into the hard and soft palate. The soft palate can seal off the airway into the nasal cavity.

Peristalsis: wave-like muscular movement that pushes food along the digestive system.

Pharynx: the throat passage through which both food and air travel.

Plasma: clear fluid in which red and white blood cells float.

Pleura: thin membrane that forms a protective covering over the lungs and lines the chest cavity.

Pulmonary artery: blood vessel through which blood is pumped from the heart to the lungs.

Respiration: chemical process in which living cells use food substances and oxygen as a source of energy, releasing carbon dioxide as a waste product.

Respiratory system: mouth, nose, pharynx, larynx, trachea, bronchi, lungs, diaphragm and intercostal muscles. The whole system is used in breathing.

Sinuses: air spaces behind the face, in the cheeks and forehead.

Sinusitis: painful blockage of the sinuses, usually caused by an infection such as a cold.

Sternum: the breastbone at the front of the chest, to which most of the ribs are attached.

Trachea: the largest airway. A short, flexible tube beginning at the larynx and supported by sections of cartilage. The two bronchi branch from the trachea.

Turbinates: another name for nasal conchae.

Uvula: soft flap at the back of the soft palate.

Vena cava: one of the two largest blood vessels in the body, bringing blood into the heart.

Virus: disease-producing organism which can live inside a cell, and it then "takes over".

Vocal cords: two tough sheets stretched across the larynx, which vibrate in the air flow, producing sounds.

Index